PATANJALI
YOGA SUTRAS

Essence and Sanskrit Grammar

Ashwini Kumar Aggarwal

Jai Gurudev

Title Patanjali Yoga Sutras
Subtitle Essence and Sanskrit Grammar

13 May 2018 Tera May, Guruji's 62nd Birthday
Masik Shivaratri, Pradosh, Trayodashi Tithi, Revati Nakshatra
Krishna Paksha, Grishma Ritu, Jyeshtha Masa, Uttarayana
Vikram Samvat 2075 Virodhakrit, Saka Samvat 1940 Vilambi

The Art of Living Center
147 Punjabi Bagh, Patiala 147001
Punjab, India

Website https://advaita56.weebly.com/
Devotees of Sri Sri Ravi Shankar Ashram

1st Edition May 2018

Jai Gurudev

Beloved Sri Sri

Master unparalleled

An offering at His Lotus feet

Jai Gurudev

ॐ

Acknowledgements

a Sanyam that reverberates with the joys of a multitude of devotees in the Yagnashala

Special Thanks

Velu Rahul KashiBhaiya KrishnaKumar Chayanna Hemswaroop
Jyoti Sivaraj Yashoda Venkatji Aruna HarjotKaur Kulwant Sarvjit
Preeti Banka Puneet Anuj Zeenu ShivaPrasad Anmol PapaMummy
Sathyavathi Sheetal Krishanjit Pinky Lalit Sanjam Pratham AmarA2

Seed sown 5/5/2018 Yagnashala
First penning 856am 16/5/2018 volvo to patiala

Front Cover Photo Credits

A trek to Parashar Lake, the ice cold -9°C snow clad mountains in Himachal Pradesh, by Dipanshu dated 27th January 2018.

Jai Gurudev

Table of Contents

Table of Topics...6

Preface 7

Blessing 8

Introduction 9

Prayer 10

Samadhi Pada 1st Quarter.......................................11

Sadhana Pada 2nd Quarter.......................................35

Vibhooti Pada 3rd Quarter......................................59

Kaivalya Pada 4th Quarter......................................83

Yoga Sutras for Chanting.......................................101

Sanskrit Word Index..109

The Sanskrit Alphabet 121

Pronunciation of Sanskrit Letters 122

Place & Effort of Enunciation 123

Devanagari Latin ISO 15919 Chart 124

References...125

Asana Pranayama 127

The Tamil Siddha Bogar 127

Agnistoma 127

Yogis in my Life 128

Epilogue 129

Table of Topics

Topic			Sutra
Samadhi Pada 1ˢᵗ Quarter - Contemplation			
Definition of Yogic Life 1.1	Ultimate Aim of a Human Birth		**1.2**
Thoughts, Impulses, Modulations, Mind-Stuff Chitta-Vritti			1.5
Abhyaasa and Vairagya to calm Impulses			**1.12**
Samadhi The Subtle Classified			1.17
Seekers			1.21
Who is God? Ishvara			1.24
A Master is Needed. Guru is of paramount importance			**1.26**
Obstacles Thorns Impediments Antaraaya			1.30
Ways to Overcome Thorns			1.32
Samadhi The Subtle Classified2			1.42
Sadhana Pada 2ⁿᵈ Quarter – The Practices			
Pointers to Yogic Life			2.1
Inimical Temperaments, Afflictions, Kleshas			2.3
Cause of Kleshas			2.12
What is this Creation?			2.18
Practices 2.26	Eight Limbs of Yoga **2.29**	Fruits of Practice	2.35
Asana 2.46	Pranayama 2.49	Pratyahara	2.54
Vibhooti Pada 3ʳᵈ Quarter – Meditation, Sanyam, Siddhi			
Dharana – Focus			3.1
Dhyana – Flow			3.2
Samadhi – Deep Meditation			3.3
Sanyam – The Trio			**3.4**
Siddhis - Attainments			3.16
Kaivalya - Divine Purity			3.55
Kaivalya Pada 4ᵗʰ Quarter - Liberation			
Causes of Attainments 4.1	Development of Minds		4.4
Action and Karma 4.7	Mindsets		4.15
Kaivalya - Living in the Center – Grace of the Divine			**4.34**

Preface

The Yoga philosophy is a fundamental text on living day to day life, on achieving success, and on preparing oneself for Liberation.

PATANJALI towers as a colossus on mankind's landscape by giving scientific treatises on YOGA, AYURVEDA and GRAMMAR. Even after achieving all sorts of progress on the mechanical front in terms of space exploration, smart cars, big infrastructures and fancy gadgets, one is left in awe of the man who could so precisely state, *literally print in words*, the unfathomable mysteries of the inner world. Unequivocally and in simple understandable language PATANJALI discusses the functioning of the brain, mind, heart; thoughts, feelings, emotions. He gives direct, easy and functional solutions for living a superfit, successful and superior life.

Out of the various aspects of mind and thinking introduced, I was especially benefitted by the concept of **Vikalpa**, **Bhranti Darshana** and **Aparigraha**. These helped clear up so much dust and cobwebs from my mind, as well as from my room and lodgings.

This is the beauty of Patanjali, he introduces one to the myriad possibilities of what the mind is doing, and one or the other shaft can strike home. As we can see, each word is pregnant with extensive meaning, containing a significant message for everyone.

Hence it is needed to go over the sutras slowly. And each time one picks up the same sutra, an enhanced or potentially useful lesson may spring forth. This involves a lot of **Tapas**, a lot of willing practice. Sufficient time and energy is to be devoted to **Asana, Pranayama** and **Meditation.** That is what will surely get you there.

In gratefulness to my Master, beloved Sri Sri, whose Meditation techniques have nourished this pristine wisdom.

Blessing

A disease-free body, a quiver-free breath, a stress-free mind, an inhibition-free intellect, an obsession-free memory, an ego that includes all, and a soul which is free from sorrow is the birthright of every human being.

```
You Are A Treasure House Of All Noble
Qualities
```

H H Sri Sri Ravi Shankar
3rd May 2018, Sanyam Session
The Art of Living Bangalore Ashram

Introduction

Maharishi Patanjali was the incarnation of Adishesha, the thousand headed protective force of Lord Narayana. His mother was named Gonika and his birth was to establish the twin pillars of Yoga and Ayurveda.

Also, he taught the Vyakarana Mahabhashya, a commentary on Panini's Ashtadhyayi, thus re-establishing the foundations of the Sanskrit Language, the day to day mode of communication.

Patanjali's Aphorisms consisting of 195 verses got classified into four chapters or quarters by his disciples
    Samadhi Pada - 51 verses, Sadhana Pada - 55 verses
    Vibhooti Pada - 55 sutras (or 56), Kaivalya Pada - 34 sutras
And it came to be known as Ashtanga Yoga, the Yoga Aphorisms consisting of Eight Limbs.

> This book follows a simple convention of separating the Sandhis, and hyphenating the Compounds, for its use as a grammar text.

The Sanskrit Language is marvellous. Each Sanskrit word is crafted with a precision that packs a world of meaning in it. Each word is like a condensed book!

Consider ॐ = प्रणवः , प्र + णु स्तुतौ + घञ् = प्रणव + सुँ = प्रणवः । Om
Special praise = sacred sound = mystic symbol = Lord

समाधि = सम् + आङ् + धि धारणे । Samadhi
Meditation = possessing evenness = being tranquil = Lordship

सूत्र literally means thread and Sutras are threads woven into a fabric that covers, protects and lends grace to the wearer. May this fabric be your shield as well as your adornment.

Traditionally a prayer is chanted before the beginning of any work or study. Since our purpose is study, we have taken a prayer that expresses gratefulness towards our Teacher.

ॐ

गुरुर्ब्रह्मा गुरुर्विष्णुः गुरुर्देवो महेश्वरः ।

गुरुः साक्षात् परं ब्रह्म तस्मै श्री गुरवे नमः ॥

In Sanskrit, the opening prayer specific to a task is called Mangalacharanam मङ्गलाचरणम् । It helps to focus one's mind on the current topic. Bringing the Mind to The Present Moment.
We recite the famous ode from the School of Yoga Philosophy.

वाक्यकारं वररुचिं भाष्यकारं पतञ्जलिम् ।

पाणिनिं सूत्रकारश्च प्रणतोऽस्मि मुनित्रयम् ॥

योगेन चित्तस्य पदेन वाचां मलं शरीरस्य च वैद्यकेन ।

योऽपाकरोतं प्रवरम मुनीनां पतञ्जलिं प्राञ्जलिरानतोऽस्मि ॥

Humble pranaams to the Sages trio, Panini who wrote the grammar sutras, Vararuchi who clarified by Vartikas and Patanjali who expounded by Bhashya.
By Yoga the pleasant mind, by Grammar the faultless speech, and by Ayurveda the fit body, he who gave, to that Rishi Patanjali, I gratefully prostrate with folded palms.

समाधिपादः samādhipādaḥ

Subtle Aspects

GRATEFULNESS. The INSPIRATION Contemplation and Preparation

अथ योगानुशासनम् । atha yogānuśāsanam । 1

अथ योग-अनुशासनम् ।

1.1 Now the Directive for a Yogic Life

Let us now see how to live a yogic life. Let us understand how to keep physically fit and mentally alert so that wisdom may dawn. We shall now study the principles to be implemented for attaining a joyous, peaceful and productive state of existence.

atha = now
yoga = life of perfection, of union with divine, being fit and capable
anuśāsanam = directive, guiding principle, self-discipline
Yogic Life = a mature, pragmatic and cheerful life. A sensible and sensitive living. Being able to shoulder responsibility, care for the society at large, and be tranquil and peaceful at the same time.

योगश्चित्तवृत्तिनिरोधः । yogaścittavṛttinirodhaḥ । 2

योगः चित्त–वृत्ति–निरोधः ।

1.2 Yogic Life entails a Calming of the Processes in the Mind

What is the definition of a Yogic Life?

A yogic life is that wherein excessive thought processes in the mind get moderated. When the work of senses is subdued, greater clarity, strength and vitality is achieved. We are thus able to live smoothly, gracefully, brilliantly.

Notice Patanjali's masterstroke right in Verse 1.2, right in the very beginning. He lays down the ultimate aim of Yoga. The sought for ideal, the hardest to attain.

And we have seen the great men and women who have walked this path and shone brilliantly in the world. Lata Mangeshkar, Sachin Tendulkar, Swami Vivekananda, Mahatma Gandhi, Einstein, Lincoln, Abdul Kalam, etc. They are great since they overcame the leaky thoughts, disturbing moods or wavering emotions, and achieved an integration of body-mind-spirit, so that their creativity and productivity shown. They rose above the vagaries of nature or man-made conflicts; and by their simple, steadfast and devout life brought solace and succour to millions around the globe. And also gladdened the hearts of many.

Refer the famous verses from Bhagavad Gita on definition of Yoga

योगस्थः कुरु कर्माणि, सङ्गं त्यक्त्वा धनञ्जय ।

सिद्ध्यसिद्ध्योस् समो भूत्वा, समत्वं योग उच्यते ॥ *2.48 Bhagavad Gita*

बुद्धियुक्तो जहातीह, उभे सुकृतदुष्कृते ।

तस्माद् योगाय युज्यस्व, योगः कर्मसु कौशलम् ॥ *2.50 Bhagavad Gita*

तदा द्रष्टुः स्वरूपेऽवस्थानम् । tadā draṣṭuḥ svarūpe'vasthānam । 3

तदा द्रष्टुः स्वरूपे अवस्थानम् ।

1.3 Then one realizes the Seer's essential Nature

By living a yogic life, we are able to get a glimpse of the ultimate reality. We are able to become one with the laws of the Universe. We can then be in harmony with the Great Forces of physics and quantum mechanics, with the currents that govern the subatomic states and also with the intergalactic events. We can identify with the creation at large.

वृत्तिसारूप्यमितरत्र । vṛttisārūpyamitaratra । 4

वृत्ति-सारूप्यम् इतरत्र ।

1.4 Else we stick to our limited MindSet

In case we do not live a yogic life, we form opinions and concepts based on our own thinking and day to day situations. We consider our own experiences as the reality. We make decisions based solely on our senses and bodily demands. We thus live just like a frog-in-the-well.

वृत्तयः पञ्चतय्यः क्लिष्टाक्लिष्टाः । vṛttayaḥ pañcatayyaḥ kliṣṭākliṣṭāḥ । 5

वृत्तयः पञ्चतय्यः क्लिष्ट-अक्लिष्टाः ।

1.5 Thoughts are FiveFold, painful or not-painful

The thinking one does can be broadly classified into five types. Each of these types may be stressful or otherwise. Here the entire range of movements, sensations, memories, feelings, and all that goes on in the mind is being classified. All possible sensory inputs, functioning, decision making, blue screen of crash, and any other thoughts are being classified.

प्रमाणविपर्ययविकल्पनिद्रास्मृतयः ।

pramāṇaviparyayavikalpanidrāsmṛtayaḥ । 6

प्रमाण-विपर्यय-विकल्प-निद्रा-स्मृतयः ।

1.6 Evident Erronous Fanciful Sleep Recollection

The FiveFold mental processes are
i) Thought Processes that are Evident, i.e. based on some truth, based on correct information.
ii) Thought Processes that are Erronous, i.e. based on error in judgement.
iii) Thought Processes that are Fanciful, i.e. imaginary
iv) Thought Processes that are Sleep, i.e. whatever is happening in sleep.

v) Thought Processes that are from Memory, i.e. those one remembers or recollects.

प्रत्यक्षानुमानागमाः प्रमाणानि । pratyakṣānumānāgamāḥ pramāṇāni । 7
प्रत्यक्ष–अनुमान–आगमाः प्रमाणानि ।

1.7 Evident includes directPerception, inferredCorrectly and basedonWellgroundedTestimony

The subtypes of the EvidentThoughtProcesses are
- directPerception
i.e. thoughts, opinions sensations arising from alert and correct sensory input. e.g. one sees a Red Traffic Signal, one hears the siren of an ambulance, drops of Rain touch the skin, etc.

- inferredCorrectly
i.e. we see smoke and infer there is a fire. we see wet roads and landscape and infer a shower of rain. we hear a loud roar from the devotees and infer that Guruji has arrived. we hear a loud applause from the crowd and infer that the home team has won.

- basedonWellgroundedTestimony
information from Scriptures, the written or spoken word that is commonly and long term accepted. information from the National Board exam results on the Net or a standard news item from a reliable Radio channel, that is generally accepted by a large populace.

विपर्ययो मिथ्याज्ञानमतद्रूपप्रतिष्ठम् ।
viparyayo mithyājñānamatadrūpapratiṣṭham । 8
विपर्ययः मिथ्या–ज्ञानम् अतद्–रूप–प्रतिष्ठम् ।

1.8 Erronous means False, based on incorrect Reasoning

An ErronousThoughtProcess is one that is formed due to some moodiness, mental bias, stubbornness or fallacious learning or false notions.

शब्दज्ञानानुपाती वस्तुशून्यो विकल्पः ।

śabdajñānānupātī vastuśūnyo vikalpaḥ । 9

शब्द–ज्ञान–अनुपाती वस्तु–शून्यः विकल्पः ।

1.9 Fanciful means caused by sound that has No basis

A FancifulThoughtProcess is one that arises from some external trigger like a word or sound or sight or smell and mixes with one's imagination to produce something totally baseless or irrelevant.

Usually happens when one has a painful memory, and one sees or hears something where some person or situation from the painful memory is present, and then one's fertile imagination works overtime to produce the Vikalpa.

Later in verse 1.30, Bhranti Darshana is listed as one of the nine obstacles. Vikalpa is very similar to Bhranti Darshana.

अभावप्रत्ययालम्बना वृत्तिर्निद्रा । abhāvapratyayālambanā vṛttirnidrā । 10

अभाव–प्रत्यय–आलम्बना वृत्तिः निद्रा ।

1.10 Sleep is when Mind is Devoid of sensory, memory or intuitive inputs

Sleep is another state in which the mind is found to be in. It is also classified under a type of ThoughtProcess, being a distinct state of mind. It is when inputs to the mind are not there. During sleep ideas are not there in the mind.

अनुभूतविषयासम्प्रमोषः स्मृतिः ।

anubhūtaviṣayāsampramoṣaḥ smṛtiḥ ‖ 11

अनुभूत–विषय–असम्प्रमोषः स्मृतिः ।

1.11 Memory is that which is solely from Past, yet that is untarnished or still unfaded

RecollectionThoughtProcess is a state of mind when one remembers something from the past. It is a reliving of an experience. It is not a forgotten incident nor is it in fragments. It is still undiluted or unaltered, e.g. I remember passing 10th std in 1981. Someone remembers that yesterday was their anniversary. She recollects that she had tomato soup for lunch.

अभ्यासवैराग्याभ्यां तन्निरोधः । abhyāsavairāgyābhyāṁ tannirodhaḥ ‖ 12

अभ्यास–वैराग्याभ्यां तत् निरोधः ।

1.12 By the twin practices of Abhyaasa and Vairagya those are Tempered

Those modulations in the mind, those thoughtProcesses, those waves and storms and impulses and ideas of the mind can be tempered by the twin practices of abhyasa = assiduousness and vairagya = dispassion. The mind can be calmed and healed and sobered by the double-edged sword of persistence and dispassion.

Five types of mental states were cognized by Patanjali in previous sutras 1.5 to 1.11, and none of these five states is the Yogic or Desirable state. By assiduity and dispassion, one may overcome the five mental states to achieve the Yogic state.

After laying down the Ultimate Aim in Verse 1.2, here in Verse 1.12 Patanjali gives the fool-proof guiding principle to attain the same.

तत्र स्थितौ यत्नोऽभ्यासः । tatra sthitau yatno'bhyāsaḥ । 13

तत्र स्थितौ यत्नः अभ्यासः ।

1.13 Abhyaasa means being Steadfast in one's Effort

The quality of Abhyaasa is defined. It is stated as the adherence to one's sadhana or yogic practices or disciplines. Being resolute, regular, unflinching and stable in one's sadhana.

स तु दीर्घकालनैरन्तर्यसत्कारासेवितो दृढभूमिः ।

sa tu dīrghakālanairantaryasatkārāsevito dṛḍhabhūmiḥ । 14

सः तु दीर्घ–काल–नैरन्तर्य–सत्कार–आसेवितः दृढ–भूमिः ।

1.14 And that when continuous over a long period of time with sincere devotion, establishes firm foundation

Our life gets the benefit of Abhyaasa only in due course of time. Our temperament becomes firm only after many years of practice. The yogic foundations become strongly rooted in our consciousness only after prolonged habit. That too when our practice is full of Sincerity and when our heart is filled with Devotion.

दृष्टानुश्रविकविषयवितृष्णस्य वशीकारसंज्ञा वैराग्यम् ।

dṛṣṭānuśravikaviṣayavitṛṣṇasya vaśīkārasaṁjñā vairāgyam । 15

दृष्ट–आनुश्रविक–विषय–वितृष्णस्य वशीकार–संज्ञा वैराग्यम् ।

1.15 Vairagya means keeping in check the feverishness that arises from sensual contact of sights and sounds

Vairagya or Dispassion is the virtue of not allowing craving to develop from objects and peoples, seen or heard or touched or smelled or tasted. Both craving and aversion are meant here. All sensual contacts or even memory or intuitive contacts are meant here. Keeping in check refers to the fact that the mind does not get affected at all. Or we can say that emotions due to sensual contacts are practically extinguished.

तत्परं पुरुषख्यातेर्गुणवैतृष्ण्यम् ।

tatparaṁ puruṣakhyātergunavaitṛṣṇyam । 16

तत्परं पुरुष-ख्यातेः गुण-वैतृष्णयम् ।

1.16 Highest state of Vairagya is Knowledge of the Self, when even the forces of nature Lose their influence

The highest state of Dispassion is when even the primeval forces of nature, i.e. hunger and thirst, or fears and angers, no longer cloud our thinking. When even the natural impulses are quenched and one gets the knowledge of the Self.

वितर्कविचारानन्दास्मितारूपानुगमात् सम्प्रज्ञातः ।

vitarkavicārānandāsmitārūpānugamāt samprajñātaḥ । 17

वितर्क–विचार–आनन्द–अस्मिता–रूप–अनुगमात् सम्प्रज्ञातः ।

1.17 Samprajnatah arises from Vitarka followed by Vichara followed by Ananda and then Asmita_of_form

The steps to achieving Samprajnatah = deliberateMeditation are
- vitarka=carefulExamination i.e. first focussing clearly on an Object
- vichārā = innerReflection i.e. then a mental Contemplation
- ānandā = joyArising i.e. then joy erupts or we feel inspired
- asmitā_of_form = Oneness i.e. finally a sense of Oneness prevails

विरामप्रत्ययाभ्यासपूर्वः संस्कारशेषोऽन्यः ।

virāmapratyayābhyāsapūrvaḥ saṁskāraśeṣo'nyaḥ । 18

विराम–प्रत्यय–अभ्यास–पूर्वः संस्कार–शेषः अन्यः ।

1.18 Another type of Meditation is due to prior_Practice that gives rise to a state of thoughtlessness, but latent impressions remain

The other, Asamprajnatah = non-deliberateMeditation occurs due to fruition of prior practices. The prior practices can be from one's past or even from the past lives. In such a case some latent tendencies will remain even though the mind feels tranquil.

भवप्रत्ययो विदेहप्रकृतिलयानाम् ।

bhavapratyayo videhaprakṛtilayānām ꠰ 19

भव–प्रत्ययः विदेह–प्रकृति–लयानाम् ।

1.19 Then there is a Samadhi of feeling bodiless and a Samadhi of being absorbed in nature

While we interact with this creation consisting of physical forms there will be moments when we feel disconnected from the body. Certainly we have had some intuitive interactions or flashes of such moments. This is another type of Samadhi. Then there are beings and departed souls whose consciousness is still here, they too can experience meditation.

Then there are times when the power of nature, viz a beautiful sunset, a radiant silvery fullmoon, waves breaking on the shore, a majestic mountain or waterfall; takes us into a trance.

श्रद्धावीर्यस्मृतिसमाधिप्रज्ञापूर्वक इतरेषाम् ।

śraddhāvīryasmṛtisamādhiprajñāpūrvaka itareṣām ꠰ 20

श्रद्धा–वीर्य–स्मृति–समाधि–प्रज्ञा–पूर्वकः इतरेषाम् ।

1.20 Whereas the normal path to Meditation is preceded by Faith, Valour, Experience and BeingStill that leads to Awareness

The previous sutra gave the technique for occasional and involuntary Meditation. This sutra gives the standard voluntary technique for Meditation.

For men and women, the following steps will lead to Meditation that nurtures Awareness
- Faith i.e. devotion and trust
- Valour i.e. a do not give up attitude
- Experience i.e. remembering the teachings of the Master or a previous blissful state
- BeingStill i.e. consciously subduing the senses

तीव्रसंवेगानामासन्नः । tīvrasaṁveganāmāsannaḥ । 21

तीव्र–संवेगानाम् आसन्नः ।

1.21 An Intense will shortens the path to Liberation

After discussing various techniques for emancipation, Patanjali says that those having a burning devotion will reach the goal quickly. Those giving Topmost Priority to spiritual practices shall attain Yoga soonest.

मृदुमध्याधिमात्रत्वात् ततोऽपि विशेषः ।

mṛdumadhyādhimātratvāt tato'pi viśeṣaḥ । 22

मृदु–मध्य–अधिमात्रत्वात् ततः अपि विशेषः ।

1.22 Also the Types are weak, average and strong

Having stated that those with a strong will to succeed shall reach the goal soonest, Patanjali identifies three types of seekers.

- *those having least priority towards sadhana,*
- *those taking out average time and efforts, and finally*
- *the ones with unflinching zeal towards sadhana.*

ईश्वरप्रणिधानाद्वा । īśvarapraṇidhānādvā । 23

ईश्वर–प्रणिधानात् वा ।

1.23 Or total surrender to the Lord

Patanjali gives solace to seekers having a weak or average will-power by stating that even total surrender to the Lord shall take one quickly to the goal. Dedicating our actions to the Lord, remembering the Lord when doing action, is enough.

The grace aspect is succinctly stated here. Grace is showered in abundance on the Grateful. That is why the path of Bhakti is said to be the easiest, utter devotion to the Lord makes us one with Him in no time.

क्लेशकर्मविपाकाशयैरपरामृष्टः पुरुषविशेष ईश्वरः ।

kleśakarmavipākāśayairaparāmṛṣṭaḥ puruṣaviśeṣa īśvaraḥ ꘶ 24

क्लेश–कर्म–विपाक–आशयैः अपरामृष्टः पुरुष–विशेषः ईश्वरः ।

1.24 Lord is that special entity who is untouched by Pain, FruitsofAction or LatentExpectation

The supreme consciousness = the highest power = the Lordship is defined in this sutra, by stating that it is special or distinct from everything else, since

- *It does not feel pain or trouble or suffering*
- *It is untouched by Action or Doership*
- *It is already full and abundant so in no case is it expecting anything whatsoever, i.e. there is no chance of latent expectations.*

तत्र निरतिशयं सर्वज्ञबीजम् । tatra niratiśayaṁ sarvajñabījam ꘶ 25

तत्र निरतिशयं सर्वज्ञ–बीजम् ।

1.25 There it has unsurpassableSupremacy and the seed of allKnowingness

There i.e. in the Lord, in that special entity, there is Omnipotence and Omniscience.
Lordship is the state of unsurpassable supremacy and all knowingness.

स पूर्वेषाम् अपि गुरुः कालेनानवच्छेदात् ।

pūrveṣām api guruḥ kālenānavacchedāt ꘶ 26

सः पूर्वेषाम् अपि गुरुः कालेन अनवच्छेदात् ।

1.26 To all who came earlier also, he alone Taught, being unlimited in Time

The Lord has been the Teacher for all beings who came earlier also, since He is beyond time. The quality of Omnipresence is added.

Obtaining the Teaching from a Guru is stated and the Traditional system of Master Disciple is recommended in this sutra.

After laying down the Ultimate Aim in Verse 1.2, the methodology to achieve it in Verse 1.12, here in Verse 1.26 finally Patanjali establishes the need for a Master. A living Guru, a Guiding Light, a friend, saint, or person from whom we may get the strength to

- Establish the Ultimate Aim with clarity in our vision
- Get the details and nitty-gritty of the Methodology that will suit us
- Obtain protection, support, and blessing to last this lifetime smoothly

A havan pot fire seems weak until you turn over a log and it starts to blaze, if you can't walk or run or climb, what can a car do? Guru gives that basic ability, he opens up that receptivity within us.

तस्य वाचकः प्रणवः । tasya vācakaḥ praṇavaḥ । 27

तस्य वाचकः प्रणवः ।

1.27 He is called Pranav

The Lord goes by the name of Pranav, i.e. the sound of breath, the sound of life, the sounds made by the winds and the waves and the fires. This sound is the familiar ॐ = Om = Aum = Omkar.

Pranav simply means special sound or mystic sound or sacred sound or sacred praise, and it is equated to the sound Om in Chandogya Upanishad and other Vedic texts.

अथ खलु य उद्गीथः स प्रणवो यः प्रणवः स उद्गीथ इत्यसौ वा आदित्य उद्गीथ एष प्रणव ॐ इति होष स्वरन्नेति ॥ 1.5.1 ॥ Chandogya Upanishad

upasarga प्र + गु स्तुतौ *dhatu +* घञ् *affix +* सुप् $^{1/1}$ = प्रणवः ।

(Root No 1035 गु स्तुतौ *of 2nd conjugation as in Siddhanta Kaumudi)*

तज्जपस्तदर्थभावनम् । tajjapastadarthabhāvanam । 28

तत् जपः तत् अर्थ–भावनम् ।

1.28 Repetition of that sprouts its meaning

A repetition of Om sprouts the qualities of the Lord within us.

Taking the name of the Lord in the form of the sound Om will illumine the Lordship within us.

ततः प्रत्यक्चेतनाधिगमोऽप्यन्तरायाभावश्च ।

tataḥ pratyakcetanādhigamo'pyantarāyābhāvaśca ꞏ 29

ततः प्रत्यक् चेतना अधिगमः अपि अन्तराय–अभावः च ।

1.29 Then the Inner_Self is revealed and also the Obstacles get removed

Chanting Om or taking the name of the Lord will reveal to us our True Self. And it will also remove the difficulties and thorns and impediments from our journey.

व्याधिस्त्यानसंशयप्रमादालस्याविरतिभ्रान्तिदर्शनालब्धभूमिकत्वानवस्थितत्वानि

चित्तविक्षेपास्तेऽन्तरायाः ।

vyādhistyānasaṃśayapramādālasyāviratibhrāntidarśanālabdhabh ūmikatvānavasthitatvāni cittavikṣepāste'ntarāyāḥ ꞏ 30

व्याधि–स्त्यान–संशय–प्रमाद–आलस्य–अविरति–भ्रान्तिदर्शन– अलब्धभूमिकत्व–अनवस्थितत्वानि चित्त–विक्षेपाः ते अन्तरायाः ।

1.30 The Obstacles are Illness, Dullness, Doubt, Negligence, Sloth, Overindulgence, Delusion, beingUnsuccessful and NotBeingAbleToMaintainSuccess

Patanjali enumerates 9 Impediments. Also called the 9 Obstacles on the spiritual path. These 9 states are the Botherations that afflict the seekers and make the progress difficult.

- vyādhi = *Illness of the body*
- styāna = *Dullness of the mind*
- saṃśaya = *Doubts, suspicions and misgivings in the heart*
- pramāda = *Negligence, i.e. not doing one's duty or doing that which is forbidden, i.e. a poor intellect*
- ālasya = *Laziness = procrastination, i.e. a poor will power*
- avirati = *Overindulgence in senses, i.e. being unable to enjoy anything because one's senses have been abused*
- bhrāntiDarśana = *Delusion or hallucination or a poor ego Similar to Vikalpa of verse 1.9*
- alabdhaBhūmikatva = *being Unsuccessful, i.e. not achieving any targets, i.e. not being able to do Sadhana at all*

- *anavasthiTatva = not being able to maintain success, i.e. having poor Yogakshema, being irregular in Sadhana*

दुःखदौर्मनस्याङ्गमेजयत्वश्वासप्रश्वासा विक्षेपसहभुवः ।

duḥkhadaurmanasyāṅgamejayatvaśvāsapraśvāsā vikṣepasahabhuvaḥ । 31

दुःख–दौर्मनस्य–अङ्गमेजयत्व–श्वास–प्रश्वासाः विक्षेप–सह–भुवः ।

1.31 Sadness Bitterness bodilyHeaviness irregularInhalation and Exhalation accompany the Obstacles

When one notices any of these symptoms, it means that one or more Obstacles are active in life. These five states are the indicators that one is facing difficulty on the path of yoga.

- duḥkha = *Sadness in the mind*
- daurmanasya = *Bitterness in the heart*
- āṅgamejayatva = *bodily Heaviness, body is out of control*
- śvāsa = *irregular Inhalation, unsteady breath*
- praśvāsā = *irregular Exhalation, being unable to relax*

तत्प्रतिषेधार्थमेकतत्त्वाभ्यासः । tatpratiṣedhārthamekatattvābhyasaḥ ।32

तत् प्रतिषेध–अर्थम् एक–तत्त्व–अभ्यासः ।

1.32 To keep these obstacles at bay, One pointed effort is recommended

To rectify the difficulties on the path of yoga, the solution is to devote one's energies to a Single objective. Putting 100% in one direction or in one task will help to Overcome the obstacles.

मैत्रीकरुणामुदितोपेक्षाणां सुखदुःखपुण्यापुण्यविषयाणां भावनातश्चित्तप्रसादनम् ।33

maitrīkaruṇāmuditopekṣāṇāṁ sukhaduḥkhapuṇyāpuṇyaviṣayāṇāṁ bhāvanātaścittaprasādanam ।

मैत्री–करुणा–मुदिता–उपेक्षाणां सुख–दुःख–पुण्य–अपुण्य–विषयाणां भावनातः चित्त–प्रसादनम् ।

1.33 By cultivating an attitude of Friendliness, Compassion, Delight, Disregard towards Happy, Sad, Righteous, evilMinded people respectively; peace of mind can be achieved

Peace of mind and subjugation of the Obstacles can also be achieved by cultivating an attitude of

- *maitrī = Friendliness towards the Sukhi = Successful and Happy people*
- *karuṇā = Compassion towards the Duḥkhi = Sad and Unsuccessful people*
- *muditā = Delight in the activities of the Righteous people*
- *upekṣā = Ignoring and disregarding the activities of the Unrighteous and evilminded people.*

प्रच्छर्दनविधारणाभ्यां वा प्राणस्य ।

pracchardanavidhāraṇābhyāṁ vā prāṇasya ꘡ 34

प्रच्छर्दन-विधारणाभ्यां वा प्राणस्य ।

1.34 Or by speciallyChanging the Breathing

This is the most potent sutra of all. Here Patanjali mentions the technique of Changing the breath patterns to achieve peace of mind and overcome the obstacles on the path of yoga.

So many yogic techniques have evolved out of this one sutra. Enlightened masters across the ages and places have taught various forms of Pranayama and breath control to achieve the state of yoga.

Stopping or retaining the breath and breaking the breathing pattern as taught by a Master, i.e. Pranayama, Mudra, Bandha.

विषयवती वा प्रवृत्तिरुत्पन्ना मनसः स्थितिनिबन्धिनी ।

viṣayavatī vā pravṛttirutpannā manasaḥ sthitinibandhinī ꘡ 35

विषयवती वा प्रवृत्तिः उत्पन्ना मनसः स्थिति–निबन्धिनी ।

1.35 Or a determined focus on any Object will Steer the mind to calmness

Children are able to keep a fresh mind and how? Because they are totally absorbed in their toy or game. The highly creative artist or scientist or engineer is able to focus fully on his talent, thus keeping his mind light.

विशोका वा ज्योतिष्मती । viśokā vā jyotiṣmatī । 36

विशोका वा ज्योतिष्मती ।

1.36 Or the Luminous_Intellect Vanquishes Sorrow

Or in the company of the one having a Brilliant Intellect, sadness is gone. Sorrow vanquishes in the presence of an enlightened Master.

We can overcome sorrow by contemplating on the Brilliant.

वीतरागविषयं वा चित्तम् । vītarāgaviṣayaṁ vā cittam । 37

वीत-राग-विषयं वा चित्तम् ।

1.37 Or a mind beyond CravingAversion

Or in the company of the one established in Vairagya, one attains peace. We can overcome obstacles by contemplating on dispassion.

स्वप्ननिद्राज्ञानालम्बनं वा । svapnanidrājñānālambanaṁ vā । 38

स्वप्न-निद्रा-ज्ञान-आलम्बनं वा ।

1.38 Or Awareness of sleep and dream states
Or in deep sleep or pleasant dream states, one attains peace.

We can overcome obstacles by becoming aware of the deep sleep state and also by becoming aware of some pleasant dreams. These states can teach us to let go.

यथाभिमतध्यानाद्वा । yathābhimatadhyānādvā । 39

यथा अभिमत-ध्यानात् वा ।

1.39 Or for instance a contemplation on the Desirable
Or by contemplation on what is desirable, one attains peace.

This is to say that since we all have varying temperaments and our situations are more or less different, hence we can employ any technique that suits us to go into Meditation, and overcome obstacles on the path.

परमाणुपरममहत्त्वान्तोऽस्य वशीकारः ।

paramāṇuparamamahattvānto'sya vaśīkāraḥ । 40

परमाणु-परम–महत्त्व–अन्तः अस्य वशीकारः ।

1.40 This leads to Mastery over the smallest and the biggest

Being established in Meditation gives the fruits of becoming friends with the atomic as well as with the galactic. Then the entire creation loves us.
We can be at ease in any situation. Whether it is an interview or an exam or a difficult situation, we can manage it well. In an AMC, we can draw very well and play games and participate in processes too enthusiastically.

क्षीणवृत्तेरभिजातस्येव मणेर्ग्रहीतृग्रहणग्राह्येषु तत्स्थतदञ्जनतासमापत्तिः ।

kṣīṇavṛtterabhijātasyeva maṇergrahītṛgrahaṇagrāhyeṣu tatsthatadañjanatāsamāpattiḥ । 41

क्षीण–वृत्तेः अभिजातस्य इव मणेः ग्रहीतृ–ग्रहण–ग्राह्येषु तत्स्थ तत् अञ्जनता समापत्तिः ।

1.41 DiminishedModulations make the mind reflect the Seer-Seeing-Seen like a high quality diamond, and that is Liberation

When the thoughtProcesses have decayed, the mind becomes like a pure reflecting crystal, and it plays the roles of Seer, Seeing and Seen effortlessly. Then the mind can be in the moment. This is liberation. This is Meditation. This is culmination of the practices. This is attaining Yoga.

TatsthaTadajanta Samaapatti = Meditation that reflects the moment clearly

तत्र शब्दार्थज्ञानविकल्पैः संकीर्णा सवितर्का समापत्तिः । (also without word तत्र)

tatra śabdārthajñānavikalpaiḥ saṁkīrṇā savitarkā samāpattiḥ । 42

तत्र शब्द–अर्थ–ज्ञान–विकल्पैः संकीर्णा सवितर्का समापत्तिः ।

1.42 Savitarka Samadhi is where awareness of sound, its meaning, and resulting wisdom are combined

savitarkā samāpattiḥ = MeditationWithReasoning = is that which combines Awareness of thoughts with meaning with external inputs.

This is the Meditation we generally experience in satsangs and during discourses. This is also the Meditation that one experiences when one sits for it.

स्मृतिपरिशुद्धौ स्वरूपशून्येवार्थमात्रनिर्भासा निर्वितर्का ।

smṛtipariśuddhau svarūpaśūnyevārthamātranirbhāsā nirvitarkā । 43

स्मृति–परिशुद्धौ स्वरूप–शून्या इव अर्थमात्र–निर्भासा निर्वितर्का ।

1.43 Nirvitarka is like being blanked out, with only a faint cognition, when memory is completely purified

nirvitarkā samāpattiḥ = MeditationWithoutReasoning = that which feels like a void due to complete purification of memory, just a faint awareness is present.

This is definitely experienced during Advanced Meditation Courses, when there is no cognition of the body or the external world, and there are no thoughts, yet an awareness persists.

एतयैव सविचारा निर्विचारा च सूक्ष्मविषया व्याख्याता ।

etayaiva savicārā nirvicārā ca sūkṣmaviṣayā vyākhyātā । 44

एतया एव सविचारा निर्विचारा च सूक्ष्म–विषयाः व्याख्याता ।

1.44 In this manner, Thoughtful and Thoughtless Meditative states have been told for Subtle Topics only

Patanjali is making it clear that Meditation, whether it is savicāra = withThoughts, or nirvicāra = withoutThoughts, is a topic of the subtle.

Nirvicara Samadhi is definitely experienced during Advanced Meditation Courses, when the mind is absolutely still, and there is no cognition of the body or the external world.

Verses 1.42 to 1.44 mention a total of four Meditative states,
Savitarka = withReasoning i.e. thoughts and sensory inputs plus intellect
Nirvitarka = withoutReasoning i.e. thoughts and inputs but no intellect
Savichara = withThoughts i.e. thoughts alone
Nirvichara = withoutThoughts i.e. nothing

Meditation is not a gross state, i.e. it is not measurable. It is only an inner state of the mind. It is only an inner state of the heart. It is something that cannot be expressed. It is not a transactional entity.

To put it another way, a lot of energy, a lot of spirit, a lot of strength, a lot of will is needed to go into Meditation. These are subtle topics and Meditation can only be experienced by a brave.

सूक्ष्मविषयत्वं चालिङ्गपर्यवसानम् ।

sūkṣmaviṣayatvaṁ cāliṅgaparyavasānam ꠰ 45

सूक्ष्म–विषयत्वं च अलिङ्ग–परि–अवसानम् ।

1.45 And of the subtle, the unManifested is the Conclusion

Meditation is a subtle topic. This was stated earlier.
The unManifested = the Lord is also a topic of the subtle, and He is the concluding topic, i.e. He is even beyond the subtle.

To put it another way, the Lord is so subtle that He cannot be described or talked about. We cannot know anything about Him.

ता एव सबीजः समाधिः । tā eva sabījaḥ samādhiḥ । 46

ताः एव सबीजः समाधिः ।

1.46 Those indeed are Samadhi with latentImpressions

The aforementioned states of Meditation are those where latent seeds or impressions will be present in the Seeker.
In all the previous verses 1.17 to 1.20, 1.32 to 1.39, 1.41 to 1.44, where Meditation has been mentioned, Patanjali is making it clear that the Meditative state may not free the soul of past impressions. However it will definitely ensure a happy trouble-free journey for the Seeker.

Possibly the impressions will also become faint, if not totally wiped out. As certified by Patanjali in the following verses.

निर्विचारवैशारद्येऽध्यात्मप्रसादः ।

nirvicāravaiśāradye'dhyātmaprasādaḥ । 47

निर्विचार–वैशारद्ये अध्यात्म–प्रसादः ।

1.47 Mastery in Thoughtless_State bestows divine Grace

When one becomes an expert in Meditation, then grace begins to shower. Meditating regularly is clearly implied here. It is the path to liberation.

ऋतम्भरा तत्र प्रज्ञा । ṛtambharā tatra prajñā । 48

ऋतम्–भरा तत्र प्रज्ञा ।

1.48 Then Awareness is filled with Truth

When one Meditates regularly, then one's awareness is full of truth. Then one's mind is flawless. One perceives the truth alone.

श्रुतानुमानप्रज्ञाभ्यामन्यविषया विशेषार्थत्वात् ।

śrutānumānaprajñābhyāmanyaviṣayā viśeṣārthatvāt । 49

श्रुत–अनुमान–प्रज्ञाभ्याम् अन्य–विषया विशेष–अर्थत्वात् ।

1.49 Specially Meaningful, it is other than Hearing or Inferential knowledge

When one Meditates regularly, then the quality of one's awareness is special. It is different from the awareness one gets solely from lectures or education or guesswork in any manner.

तज्जः संस्कारोऽन्यसंस्कारप्रतिबन्धी ।

tajjaḥ saṁskāro'nyasaṁskārapratibandhī । 50

तत् जः संस्कारः अन्य–संस्कार–प्रतिबन्धी ।

1.50 The Impression born of this Overrides other impressions

Meditation produces an impression that overwrites the earlier impressions. This is clearly felt by the seeker who meditates regularly. The mind becomes clear by and by.

तस्यापि निरोधे सर्वनिरोधान्निर्बीजः समाधिः ।

tasyāpi nirodhe sarvanirodhānnirbījaḥ samādhiḥ । 51

तस्य अपि निरोधे सर्व–निरोधात् निर्बीजः समाधिः ।

1.51 The Samadhi without Latent Impressions is achieved when even this is dropped

A day comes when all impressions have been overwritten or wiped out. Patanjali states this slightly differently, in the sense that such happens involuntarily some day. Grace is the key.

|| ~~~ ||

Who are you fooling?

I have no time. You certainly have more than enough time, but **you have no patience.**

I cannot spare the cash. You are spending tons on medicines, tuition and gadgetry. **You simply have your priorities mixed up.**

My boss is difficult. My spouse does not agree to it. When was the last time you had a sensible conversation? **You are terrible in confidence.**

You cannot even wake up. You cannot even go for a long walk. **Are you even alive?**

My app doesn't release me. **You are enslaved Royally.**

Face the Facts.

Life is Precious. You have been blessed by a human birth. You have a superb body, an amazing intellect and a wonderful spirit. **Put it to the best use. Give 100%.**

Patanjali Yoga Sutras

पातञ्जलयोगसूत्राणि

Pātañjalayogasūtrāṇi

पातञ्जल-योग-सूत्राणि

Pātañjala-Yoga-Sūtrāṇi

The spelling पातञ्जल is the correct Sanskrit spelling using a taddhita affix when used in the sense "of Patañjali" पतञ्जलेः [6/1] in a compound word. Whereas spelling of Patañjali standing alone is पतञ्जलिः [1/1] । The stem is पतञ्जलि [m] = पतॄ गतौ + अञ्जलि । The one who fell in the cupped palms of his mother at birth. The one who offered himself for the salvation of mankind.

साधनपादः sādhanapādaḥ

Practical Aspects

SUDARSHAN KRIYA, GURU PUJA, AGNIHOTRA
The Practice, Techniques, Methods

तपःस्वाध्यायेश्वरप्रणिधानानि क्रियायोगः ॥ १ ॥

tapaḥsvādhyāyeśvarapraṇidhānāni kriyāyogaḥ ॥ 1 ॥

तपः–स्वाध्याय–ईश्वरप्रणिधानानि क्रिया–योगः ।

2.1 Tapas, Svadhyaya and Ishvarpranidhana are directives for Yoga

Sadhana for the seeker constitutes of
- tapaḥ = going wilfully through discipline and practice, having forbearance. *Compare titiksha of Shat Sampati or 6 Wealths from Adi Sankaracharya.*
- svādhyāya = self study, devoting enough time and priority to personal sadhana, study of scripture and correct dinacharya that suits one's constitution.
- īśvarapraṇidhāna = total surrender to the Lord, acknowledging the presence of a higher power, acknowledging the support of nature and its forces, being devoted to the Master

समाधिभावनार्थः क्लेशतनूकरणार्थश्च ॥२॥

samādhibhāvanārthaḥ kleśatanūkaraṇārthaśca ॥2॥

समाधि–भावनार्थः क्लेश–तनू–करणार्थः च ।

2.2 Should be practiced for achieving Samadhi and for attenuating the Kleshas

kleśa = *inimical tendency, inner conflict*
Sadhana = Kriya yoga = discipline in life = Directive
Directives stated in Verse 2.1 should be practiced for attaining the state of Deep Meditation, AND for gradually easing out the inner conflicts.

अविद्यास्मितारागद्वेषाभिनिवेशाः क्लेशाः ॥३॥

avidyāsmitārāgadveṣābhiniveśāḥ kleśāḥ ॥3॥

अविद्या–अस्मिता–राग–द्वेष–अभिनिवेशाः क्लेशाः ।

2.3 Five kleshas are Avidya, Asmita, Raga, Dvesha and Abhinivesha

The inimical mental states or proclivities that hinder growth
avidyā = ignorance, asmitā = ego of mineness
rāga = lust, dveṣa = hate, abhiniveśa = fear of death

Whereas 9 obstacles – antaraya in the form of thorns were said earlier in verse 1.30, kleshas are not simply thorns nay these are the basic temperaments. Klesha = principal and Antaraya = interest.

अविद्याक्षेत्रमुत्तरेषां प्रसुप्ततनुविच्छिन्नोदाराणाम् ॥४॥

avidyākṣetramuttareṣāṃ prasuptatanuvicchinnodārāṇām ॥4॥

अविद्या–क्षेत्रम्–उत्तरेषां प्रसुप्त–तनु–विच्छिन्न–उदाराणाम् ।

2.4 Avidya is the primary platform for the others. Kleshas may be dormant, mild, irregular or fully active

अनित्याशुचिदुःखानात्मसु नित्यशुचिसुखात्मख्यातिरविद्या ॥ ५ ॥

anityāśuciduḥkhānātmasu nityaśucisukhātmakhyātiravidyā ॥5॥

अनित्य–अशुचि–दुःख–अनात्मसु नित्य–शुचि–सुख–आत्म–ख्यातिः अविद्या ।

2.5 Avidya causes one to consider changeable as eternal, impure as pure, painful as pleasant, and unreality as the self

दृग्दर्शनशक्त्योरेकात्मतेवास्मिता ॥ ६ ॥

dr̥gdarśanaśaktyorekātmatevāsmitā ॥6॥

दृक्–दर्शन–शक्त्योः एकात्मता इव अस्मिता ।

2.6 Asmita causes one to identify one's intellect as supreme and one's sight and things seen as infallible

सुखानुशायी रागः ॥ ७ ॥ sukhānuśayī rāgaḥ ॥7॥

सुख–अनुशयी रागः ।

2.7 Raga is dwelling on pleasure

Raga is the result of identifying with pleasures as supreme.
The thought_Process that gets born by assuming comforts as Truth.
Raga is not a spoken word. Neither is it a physical act of eating something or touching something.
Rather, raga is the mental rumination regarding comforts and pleasures. It is the imagining and day dreaming of getting things or peoples or their attention.

दुःखानुशायी द्वेषः ॥ ८ ॥ duḥkhānuśayī dveṣah ॥8॥

दुःख–अनुशयी द्वेषः ।

2.8 Dvesha is dwelling on pain

Dvesha is the result of identifying harm or pain as the ultimate. Getting stuck to hurt and guilt. The thought_Process that gets born by assuming painful events as True.

Dvesha is not the spoken word nor the action born of hatred. Rather it is the mental ruminations regarding pains and hurts from peoples and situations. It is the playing of a terrible incident again and again in the mind, or remembering a hateful person.

TV serials are made to specifically nourish Dvesha or Raga, know it forthwith and drop them like hot coals. Media and advertisement in some cases capitalize on such facets of one's personality and make it a big business, a regular money spinner.

स्वरसवाही विदुषोऽपि तथारूढोऽभिनिवेशः ॥९॥

svarasavāhī viduṣo'pi tathārūḍho'bhiniveśaḥ ॥9॥

स्व–रस–वाही विदुषः अपि तथा रूढः अभिनिवेशः ।

2.9 Abhinivesha is an inborn quality that assails the Ignorant as well as the Wise

abhiniveśa = The fear of death is actually a primeval instinct in all of us for self preservation. It is that which prevents us from being rash, from jumping off the cliff, from being an unnecessary hero. It is this that induces in us a protection towards small children.

ते प्रतिप्रसवहेयाः सूक्ष्माः ॥१०॥ te pratiprasavaheyāḥ sūkṣmāḥ ॥10॥

ते प्रतिप्रसव–हेयाः सूक्ष्माः ।

2.10 The kleshas are very subtle. These are to be dropped by conscious counter efforts

e.g. Challenge avidya with vidya in the presence of a master.
Overcome asmita by sharing and generosity.
Quell lust with falling in love with nature itself.
Avoid hate similarly by acknowleging the power of natural forces.
Minimize abhinivesha by knowing the eternal spirit.

ध्यानहेयास्तद्वृत्तयः ॥ ११ ॥ dhyānaheyāstadvṛttayaḥ ॥ 11 ॥

ध्यान–हेयाः तत् वृत्तयः ।

2.11 Dhyana will alleviate these impulses

Sitting for meditation will loosen the hold of kleshas. It will weaken the thought_Processes of the inimical forces.
Meditation is the best soap for the mind and its tendencies. It is the best detergent for keeping the mind clean and the heart supple and soft.

क्लेशमूलः कर्माशयो दृष्टादृष्टजन्मवेदनीयः ॥ १२ ॥

kleśamūlaḥ karmāśayo dṛṣṭādṛṣṭajanmavedanīyaḥ ॥ 12 ॥

क्लेश–मूलः कर्म–आशयः दृष्ट–अदृष्ट–जन्म–वेदनीयः ।

2.12 Kleshas arise from impressions of karmic forces. They get activated in the Present, or at some Future time, or even in the Next life

Inimical temperaments are formed from latent impressions.

सति मूले तद्विपाको जात्यायुर्भोगाः ॥ १३ ॥

sati mūle tadvipāko jātyāyurbhogāḥ ॥ 13 ॥

सति मूले तत् विपाकः जाति–आयुः–भोगाः ।

2.13 Due to the roots of impressions we take birth, live a lifetime, and get various experiences in life

ते ह्लादपरितापफलाः पुण्यापुण्यहेतुत्वात् ॥ १४ ॥

te hlādaparitāpaphalāḥ puṇyāpuṇyahetutvāt ॥ 14 ॥

ते ह्लाद–परिताप–फलाः पुण्य–अपुण्य–हेतुत्वात् ।

2.14 They give results as pleasure or pain, based on virtuous or sinful acts

परिणामतापसंस्कारदुःखैर्गुणवृत्तिविरोधाच्च दुःखमेव सर्वं विवेकिनः ॥ १५ ॥

pariṇāmatāpasaṃskāraduḥkhairguṇavṛttivirodhācca duḥkhameva
sarvaṃ vivekinaḥ ॥ 15 ॥

परिणाम–ताप–संस्कार–दुःखैः गुण–वृत्ति–विरोधात् च दुःखम् एव सर्वं विवेकिनः ।

2.15 The wise consider it all as only painful, whether they be fruits or thorns or impressions, and it is all contradictory

For a wise man, both pains and pleasures are actually disturbing since they will give rise to anguish and hope in turn.

हेयं दुःखमनागतम् ॥ १६ ॥ heyaṃ duḥkhamanāgatam ॥ 16 ॥

हेयं दुःखम् अनागतम् ।

2.16 Strive to Prevent pain before it comes

Right now strive hard to neutralize the future karmic balance. Make it your top priority to defend against the miseries of old age. Invest your time and efforts in procuring shelter from the inclement weather and the chance of rain. Direct your efforts accordingly.

द्रष्टृदृश्ययोः संयोगो हेयहेतुः ॥ १७ ॥

draṣṭṛdṛśyayoḥ saṃyogo heyahetuḥ ॥ 17 ॥

द्रष्टृ–दृश्ययोः संयोगः हेय–हेतुः ।

2.17 Identification of the Seer with the Seen brings misery, the cause of that is to be prevented

Misery is the result of identifying oneself with the events and peoples around us. Pain results from connecting the pure Self to the impurities around us in the form of emotions and situations. This is to be prevented at all costs. That which causes this identity is to be dropped forthwith.

Keep a strict watch on the mind because it lingers on the invalid connections caused by sight and sound. The natural tendency of the mind is to grab what we see and what we hear and give it undue importance and truth. This is to be filtered out.

प्रकाशक्रियास्थितिशीलं भूतेन्द्रियात्मकं भोगापवर्गार्थं दृश्यम् ॥१८॥

prakāśakriyāsthitiśīlaṁ bhūtendriyātmakaṁ bhogāpavargārthaṁ dṛśyam ॥18॥

प्रकाश–क्रिया–स्थिति–शीलं भूत–इन्द्रिय–आत्मकं भोग–अपवर्गार्थं दृश्यम् ।

2.18 ObjectsSeen have characteristics of Manifestation, Action and Immobility. Inputs to the senses are the Elements. The aimOfCreation is to experience and get liberated

विशेषाविशेषलिङ्गमात्रालिङ्गानि गुणपर्वाणि ॥१९॥

viśeṣāviśeṣaliṅgamātrāliṅgāni guṇaparvāṇi ॥19॥

विशेष–अविशेष–लिङ्गमात्र–अलिङ्गानि गुण–पर्वाणि ।

2.19 Creation has the attributes of Describable, Undescribable, Distinct and Indistinct

Guna = Trilogy that supports creation, viz. Sattva-Rajas-Tamas.
Parvani = Layers or Segments of the Trilogy, viz. Matter-Energy

द्रष्टा दृशिमात्रः शुद्धोऽपि प्रत्ययानुपश्यः ॥२०॥

draṣṭā dṛśimātraḥ śuddho'pi pratyayānupaśyaḥ ॥20॥

द्रष्टा दृशि–मात्रः शुद्धः अपि प्रत्यय–अनुपश्यः ।

2.20 The Seer is Only_a_Witness and Pure also, yet sees Through the Modulations

The truth or divinity within each one of us is a 'static entity'. It is simply a Witness. It is simply Purity personified.
Due to the arrangement of this creation, i.e. due to the makeup of man with his packaging, the Divinity observes through the limited Mindset. The Infinity sees through the window of the mind and the senses, as this is the way the house is constructed.

तदर्थ एव दृश्यस्यात्मा ॥ २१ ॥ tadartha eva dṛśyasyātmā ॥21॥
तदर्थ एव दृश्यस्य आत्मा ।

2.21 Creation is solely for the Seer

The construction of this creation, and the arrangements of its components, and its design, it is only for the Divine.

To put it another way, the Divine has manifested in the form of this universe. It is the Lord in the objects and peoples we see and touch. His aim is for us to realize and become free.

कृतार्थं प्रति नष्टमप्यनष्टं तदन्यसाधारणत्वात्॥ २२ ॥

kṛtārthaṁ prati naṣṭamapyanaṣṭaṁ tadanyasādhāraṇatvāt॥22॥
कृतार्थं प्रति नष्टम् अपि अनष्टं तत् अन्य-साधारणत्वात् ।

2.22 For one who has discovered the meaning, this creation disappears. For the others it is yet commonplace.

The creation evaporates for the Saint or the Realized soul. The trials and tribulations no longer exist for the Liberated.

For the rest of us, for us still busy unravelling the mystery, for the seeker still finding his way out, the caves and dungeons and sounds and sights appear Solid and Real.

A very potent and meaningful verse. Patanjali is saying that the miseries and difficulties are imaginary or unreal. He is pointing out the state of mind of the one who has cleared the examination.

स्वस्वामिशक्त्योः स्वरूपोपलब्धिहेतुः संयोगः ॥ २३ ॥

svasvāmiśaktyoḥ svarūpopalabdhihetuḥ saṁyogaḥ ॥23॥
स्व-स्वामि-शक्त्योः स्व-रूप-उपलब्धि-हेतुः संयोगः ।

2.23 The Conjunction of the Boss with his Persona is to highlight the Boss's TrueNature

And why this duality? Why is there a Master and his Shakti? Why do we have the Sun and its Shade? Why is there Light and its Heat?

Patanjali says it is for the Self to realize its True nature. The contrast is there so that the Truth be Seen.

तस्य हेतुरविद्या ॥ २४ ॥ tasya heturavidyā ॥24॥
तस्य हेतुः अविद्या ।

2.24 Avidya is its Cause

avidyā = Ignorance = Not being able to Understand is the cause of the duality.

Not being able to perceive the truth is the Cause of misery. Being unable to see the bigger picture, being unable to come out of one's shoes is the cause of pain. Being opinionated, being polarized, being stuck is the cause of misery. Ignorance is being small-minded.

तदभावात् संयोगाभावो हानं तद् दृशेः कैवल्यम् ॥ २५ ॥

tadabhāvāt saṁyogābhāvo hānaṁ tad dṛśeḥ kaivalyam ॥25॥

तत् अभावात् संयोग–अभावः हानं तत् दृशेः कैवल्यम् ।

2.25 The Absence of Identification due to Disappearance of That, is Kaivalyam, the Liberation of the Seer

Kaivalyam = absolute Detachment = infinite Bliss
The absence_of_identification_with_the_seen arises due to the disappearance_of_Avidya. This is the state of Kaivalyam. This is the Liberation of the Seer.

When one loses association with peoples and situations, then guilts and blames and fears also disappear. It is primarily the Contact of senses with their objects that leads to all types of Confusion, apprehension, dilemma and doubt. Once this Contact ceases, the Confusion also vanishes.

विवेकख्यातिरविप्लवा हानोपायः ॥ २६ ॥

vivekakhyātiraviplavā hānopāyaḥ ॥26॥

विवेक-ख्यातिः अविप्लवा हान-उपायः ।

2.26 Uninterrupted practice of Viveka is the Remedy for Removal

Well established Viveka by continuous practice is the remedy to remove the Avidya.

viveka = Discrimination = Knowing what is temporary and what is permanent = knowing that things and peoples and situations will change, yet there is something that doesn't change.

तस्य सप्तधा प्रान्तभूमिः प्रज्ञा ॥ २७ ॥

tasya saptadhā prāntabhūmiḥ prajñā ॥27॥

तस्य सप्तधा प्रान्त-भूमिः प्रज्ञा ।

2.27 Awareness comprises of a SevenTierRise to the FinalState

The final state of Awareness attained by the Yogi or the Enlightened comprises of seven sequential steps.

In the Yoga Philosphy, 7 principal chakras or subtle energy centers have been accepted. The Awareness of the highest state is when energy has established itself firmly in the 7th Chakra, the Sahasrara.

योगाङ्गानुष्ठानादशुद्धिक्षये ज्ञानदीप्तिराविवेकख्यातेः ॥ २८ ॥

yogāṅgānuṣṭhānādaśuddhikṣaye jñānadīptirāvivekakhyāteḥ ॥28॥

योग-अङ्ग-अनुष्ठानात् अशुद्धि-क्षये ज्ञान-दीप्तिः आ-विवेक-ख्यातेः ।

2.28 By practice of the LimbsOfYoga, Impurities get removed, knowledge is illuminated upto full Awareness

The discipline of Yogic practices destroys the impurities, thus making knowledge shine forth and arrive at full Awareness.

यमनियमासनप्राणायामप्रत्याहारधारणाध्यानसमाधयोऽष्टावङ्गानि ॥ २९ ॥

yamaniyamāsanaprāṇāyāmapratyāhāradhāraṇādhyānasamādhay o'ṣṭāvaṅgāni ॥29॥

यम–नियम–आसन–प्राणायाम–प्रत्याहार–धारणा–ध्यान–समाधयः अष्टौ–अङ्गानि ।

2.29 Eight Limbs are Yama, Niyama, Asana, Pranayama, Partyahara, Dharana, Dhyana and Samadhi

- yama = *Social Etiquettes = Observances in company*
- niyama = *Personal Etiquettes = Observances in private*
- āsana = *Bodily Postures*
- prāṇāyāma = *Breath Control*
- pratyāhāra = *Senses Control, turning the senses inwards*
- dhāraṇā = *Fixing the Mental Focus*
- dhyāna = *contemplation = a Thought that illumines repeatedly, where the mind goes again and again*
- samādhi = *deep Meditation = Dissolving = Absorption in Infinity*

These are the limbs of Yoga, the Divine path. Limbs because each helps the other, being steady in anyone will strengthen the others also.

Note – compare Pratyahara with the Pratyaharas of Maheshwara Sutras from Ashtadhyayi of Panini. There the word Pratyahara means a cluster, an abbreviation.

So as a grammatical term it means a contraction of letters whereas here it refers to contraction of senses.

अहिंसासत्यास्तेयब्रह्मचर्यापरिग्रहा यमाः ॥३०॥

ahiṁsāsatyāsteyabrahmacaryāparigrahā yamāḥ ॥30॥

अहिंसा–सत्य–अस्तेय–ब्रह्मचर्य–अपरिग्रहाः यमाः ।

2.30 Ahimsa, Satya, Asteya, Brahmacharya, Aprigraha are the Yamas

Yamas consist of the Social Etiquettes and Observances to be enforced when moving in company, and are five in number.
- *ahiṁsa = Non-violence in Thought, Speech and Action*
- *satya = Truthfulness = not something spoken, but something meant with good intention. Something that is aimed not to hurt. A word or action that is directed to help someone.*
- *asteya = Non-stealing = not stealing objects and also not harbouring thoughts of acquiring someone's fame or talents.*
- *brahmacarya = moving in the Brahman = moving in the infinity = Purity = loosly translated as chastity*
- *aparigraha = Non-receiving = Non-covetousness = not hoarding objects and Non-hoarding of thoughts and emotions generated by someone, not being greedy, not wishing for nor accepting gifts*

जातिदेशकालसमयानवच्छिन्नाः सार्वभौमा महाव्रतम् ॥३१॥

jātideśakālasamayānavacchinnāḥ sārvabhaumā mahāvratam ॥31॥

जाति–देश–काल–समय–अनवच्छिन्नाः सार्वभौमाः महाव्रतम् ।

2.31 Being Uninterrupted by Race, Place, Time or Occasion; and being Universal; is a huge Obligation

Yama is a fundamental duty of the seeker, and it must be Independent of
- *jāti = Race or Culture or Position in Society*
- *deśa = Place or Country*
- *kāl = Time or Season*
- *samaya = Occasion or Situation*

i.e. Yamas must be observed universally and without a break.

शौचसन्तोषतपःस्वाध्यायेश्वरप्रणिधानानि नियमाः ॥३२॥

śaucasantoṣatapaḥsvādhyāyeśvarapraṇidhānāni niyamāḥ ॥32॥

शौच–सन्तोष–तपः–स्वाध्याय–ईश्वरप्रणिधानानि नियमाः ।

2.32 Shaucha, Santosha, Tapas, Svadhyaya, Ishvarpranidhana are the Niyamas

Niyamas consist of the Personal Etiquettes and Observances to be enforced when in private

- śauca = *Cleanliness in Body, Speech and Thought = having regular bath, brushing teeth twice a day, cutting nails, combing hair, wearing clean clothes; abstaining from foul language; not harbouring ill-will*
- santoṣa = *Contentedness = like Samadhan of ShatSampati_SixWealths of Advanced Meditation Course*
- tapaḥ = *Endurance = Forbearance = Being able to follow discipline willingly = like Titiksha of ShatSampati_SixWealths of Advanced Meditation Course*
- svādhyāya = *Self Study = Devoting sufficient time and effort in Scriptures, Rituals and Self Reflection, Spending time with the Master in Satsang*
- īśvarapraṇidhāna = *Devotion = Surrender to Divine = Acknowledging a Higher Power = being soaked in Gratefulness*

वितर्कबाधने प्रतिपक्षभावनम् ॥३३॥

vitarkabādhane pratipakṣabhāvanam ॥33॥

वितर्क–बाधने प्रतिपक्ष–भावनम् ।

2.33 Defy the Obstacles by Nourishing Counter Thoughts

Keep the impediments to YogicLife at bay by encouraging and generating positive counter emotions in the heart. Many times we are stuck in our proclivities. Patanjali offers an easy way out. Simply start doing the opposite he says.

*e.g. the mind does not want to wake up at 4am and go for a walk.
So take the help of a friend to shake yourself up.
e.g. the mind is avoiding an Advanced Meditation Course. Seek the
help of your boss or spouse to send you there.
Note that the 9 Obstacles have been mentioned earlier by Patanjali
in verse 1.30, simultaneously the 5 Symptoms are listed in verse
1.31, and the 5 Proclivities are given in verse 2.3.*

*Here Patanjali uses the single word Vitarka = Special Logic in the
Mind, to refer to the Obstacles or Proclivities. He is in a way saying
that a weak will or an infirm mind is the sum-total of all difficulties.
That alone if addressed can pave the way for liberation.*

वितर्का हिंसादयः कृतकारितानुमोदिता लोभक्रोधमोहपूर्वका मृदुमध्याधिमात्रा
दुःखाज्ञानानन्तफला इति प्रतिपक्षभावनम् ॥३४॥

vitarkā himsādayaḥ kṛtakāritānumoditā lobhakrodhamohapūrvakā
mṛdumadhyādhimātrā duḥkhājñānānantaphalā iti
pratipakṣabhāvanam ‖34‖

वितर्काः हिंसादयः कृत–कारित–अनुमोदिताः लोभ–क्रोध–मोह–पूर्वकाः मृदु–
मध्य–अधिमात्राः दुःख–अज्ञान–अनन्त–फलाः इति प्रतिपक्ष–भावनम् ।

**2.34 Vitarkas manifest as Violence or Harm, whether
Committed_Caused_or_Approved, due to
Greed_Anger_or_Infatuation, in
Mild_Average_or_Serious_form, and the outcome is
Innumerable_Sorrows_and_Delusions. Therefore Nourish
Counter Thoughts.**

*Patanjali stresses the need to generate counter thoughts and
emotions in the mind by stating the consequences otherwise.
Our mind is used to thinking in a particular manner. It is unable to
tread the path of Yoga. The mind dreams up one or more reasons to
avoid waking up early or maintain the sadhana or do any good
deeds that will stand us in good stead.*

So take counter measures by awakening suitable positive thoughts.
It is a must, or else we shall fall prey to a transgression.
Unknowingly or knowingly we shall cause a blunder and create
endless hardships for ourselves and our family and friends.

अहिंसाप्रतिष्ठायां तत्सन्निधौ वैरत्यागः ॥३५॥

ahiṁsāpratiṣṭhāyāṁ tatsannidhau vairatyāgaḥ ॥35॥

अहिंसा–प्रतिष्ठायां तत् सन्निधौ वैर–त्यागः ।

2.35 Steadfastness_in_Ahimsa causes animosity to Vanish in one's vicinity

When one becomes established in Non-violence, then peoples and
events lose the chance of harming us. This is the fruit of Ahimsa.

Even ferocious animals and inclement weather conditions will
leave him untouched.

सत्यप्रतिष्ठायां क्रियाफलाश्रयत्वम् ॥३६॥

satyapratiṣṭhāyāṁ kriyāphalāśrayatvam ॥36॥

सत्य–प्रतिष्ठायां क्रिया–फल–आश्रयत्वम् ।

2.36 Steadfastness_in_Satya produces Success in Action

When one becomes established in Truth, then success is attained in
our projects and endeavours. This is the fruit of Truthfulness.

Many times companies and individuals are unable to complete
their assignments. This is due to the lack of truth.

अस्तेयप्रतिष्ठायां सर्वरत्नोपस्थानम् ॥३७॥

asteyapratiṣṭhāyāṁ sarvaratnopasthānam ॥37॥

अस्तेय–प्रतिष्ठायां सर्व–रत्न–उपस्थानम् ।

2.37 Steadfastness_in_Asteya showers all Wealths

When one becomes established in Non-stealing, then he finds many gems and treasures. This is the fruit of Non-thievery, of not cheating.

It means that for the one who does not rob, who shuns even envy or acquiring anyone's talents, many hidden fortunes await him.

ब्रह्मचर्यप्रतिष्ठायां वीर्यलाभः ॥ ३८ ॥

brahmacaryapratiṣṭhāyāṁ vīryalābhaḥ ॥38॥

ब्रह्मचर्य–प्रतिष्ठायां वीर्य–लाभः ।

2.38 Steadfastness_in_Brahmacharya grants Vital strength

When one becomes established in Purity, then vital strength is gained. This is the fruit of Chastity.

As we all know, the path of Yoga is for the Brave. It is not for the faint-hearted. Just as a rocket needs enough boosters to get into outer space, similarly one who wants to turn his senses inwards needs a great deal of vitality.

This is the power of the Enlightened Master. He can give the Shakti-path, he can make the devotee unite with the Divine.

अपरिग्रहस्थैर्ये जन्मकथन्तासम्बोधः ॥ ३९ ॥

aparigrahasthairye janmakathantāsambodhaḥ ॥39॥

अपरिग्रह–स्थैर्ये जन्म–कथन्ता–सम्बोधः ।

2.39 Steadfastness_in_Aprigraha awakens the How and Why of life

When one becomes established in Non-covetousness, then knowledge of births is illumined. This is the fruit of Non-hoarding.

Covetousness is a very sublime and subtle trait. It is hard to isolate. Unknowingly we covet someone's riches or position or fame. We even latch on to their emotions and store their praises or insults. Without thinking we receive gifts and presents during festivals and occasions. In that we also assimilate their thoughts and intentions.

And we make our mind like a movie player, we remember and relive pleasurable as well as nasty events. This inadvertently fills our memory and lowers our capacity to discern the words of the Master. There is no longer any place for wisdom as our brain is already crowded. Our harddisk is out of swap space. Our smartphone is low on resources.

Covetousness is more common than assumed. Drop it.

शौचात् स्वाङ्गजुगुप्सा परैरसंसर्गः ॥ ४० ॥

śaucāt svāṅgajugupsā parairasaṁsargaḥ ॥40॥

शौचात् स्व–अङ्ग–जुगुप्सा परैः असंसर्गः ।

2.40 Steadfastness_in_Shaucha withdraws one from own body and disconnects from others

When one becomes established in Cleanliness, then identification with the gross is shelved. This is the fruit of Hygiene.

We rarely think twice before touching or hugging, but we fail to notice that it weakens our aura aswell. Need for too much physical contact is prevented when we start to be spick and span ourselves.

Keeping our environs clean, keeping our mat and clothes clean, keeping our furniture, washroom, kitchen and bed tidy helps prevent illnesses on many levels. (apparently this is one thing the indians forgot while the europeans excelled in). The magic it does is not immediately apparent, but it keeps our wits and turns our attention away from bodies and objects, towards the divine.

सत्त्वशुद्धिसौमनस्यैकाग्र्येन्द्रियजयात्मदर्शनयोग्यत्वानि च ॥४१॥

sattvaśuddhisaumanasyaikāgryendriyajayātmadarśanayogyatvāni
ca ॥41॥

सत्त्वशुद्धि–सौमनस्य–एकाग्र्य–इन्द्रियजय–आत्मदर्शन–योग्यत्वानि च ।

**2.41 And SattvaShuddhi, Cheerfulness, One Pointedness,
Conquest of Senses, and Fitness for Realization_of_the_Self**

*Cleanliness is truly a magnificient virtue. Cleanliness in body,
speech, action and environs additionally bestows*
- *sattvaśuddhi = the Sattva guna triumphs over Tamas*
- *saumanasya = Cheerfulness, pleasant state of mind, a
  positive attitude*
- *ekāgrya = One Pointedness, so essential for success in task*
- *indriyajaya = Victory over Senses, not letting senses rule*
- *ātmadarśan yogyatva = qualifies one to tread the spiritual
  path, brings the Guru into one's life*

सन्तोषादनुत्तमसुखलाभः ॥४२॥ santoṣādanuttamasukhalābhaḥ ॥42॥

सन्तोषात् अनुत्तम–सुख–लाभः ।

2.42 From Santosha comes unparalleled Joy

santoṣa = Contentedness. It grants unmatched joy, delight, ecstasy

*It is so easy to forget that desires are unending, each desire fulfilled
gives rise to a new desire. Only when contentment is there can one
experience true happiness.*

कायेन्द्रियसिद्धिरशुद्धिक्षयात्तपसः ॥४३॥

kāyendriyasiddhiraśuddhikṣayāttapasaḥ ॥43॥

काय–इन्द्रिय–सिद्धिः अशुद्धि–क्षयात् तपसः ।

**2.43 Tapas results in body-Mind dexterity by destroying
Impurity**

tapasa = Forbearance destroys the impurities of the body and the mind. It flushes the toxins from the system, thereby one's organs and senses perform so much better.

Our body becomes really fit by even a little discipline, adherence to sadhana, as vouchsafed by so many devotees.

स्वाध्यायादिष्टदेवतासम्प्रयोगः ॥४४॥

svādhyāyādiṣṭadevatāsamprayogaḥ ॥44॥

स्वाध्यायात् इष्ट–देवता–सम्प्रयोगः ।

2.44 By Svadhyaya we get united with our Ideal

svādhyāya = Self Study = giving time to Scriptures, Rituals, Japa, Satsang unites us with our Hero. Brings us close to our Master.

iṣṭadevatā samprayoga = chosen diety manifests = the spiritual attributes we closely identify with get ripened in us.

समाधिसिद्धिरीश्वरप्रणिधानात् ॥४५॥

samādhisiddhirīśvarapraṇidhānāt ॥45॥

समाधि–सिद्धिः ईश्वर–प्रणिधानात् ।

2.45 By Ishvarpranidhana we get proficiency in Meditation

īśvarapraṇidhāna = Surrender to the Divine = absolute Devotion = Gratefulness gives us the knack to Meditate effortlessly. Gratefulness is the key. The more grateful we are, more grace flows in our life, making it smooth and pleasant.

स्थिरसुखमासनम् ॥४६॥ sthirasukhamāsanam ॥46॥

स्थिर–सुखम् आसनम् ।

2.46 Asana is that which is Stable and Comfortable
āsana = Posture is that which is firm and pleasant
It is the body pose that one can balance without strain.

A good Asana practice should include warmups e.g. walking, with

- *Surya Namaskar*
- *Padmasadhana*

प्रयत्नशैथिल्यानन्तसमापत्तिभ्याम् ॥४७॥

prayatnaśaithilyānantasamāpattibhyām ॥47॥

प्रयत्न–शैथिल्य–अनन्त–समापत्तिभ्याम् ।

2.47 Done by judicious Effort and setting the mind on the Infinite

Asana posture can be maintained by first putting in proper Effort and then Letting Go, and by remembering the Infinity. By slight effort and remembering the divine, asana becomes steady and pleasant.

Actually the body can very well do it, only the mind starts to fidget.

Knowing this Patanjali gives us the key to become proficient in our Asana practice. He says to maintain the balance become aware of 3 principles

- *Flexibility*
- *Strength*
- *The Eternal*

Many devotees have been able to hold the Asana properly by doing a japa of the sacred syllable 'Ram'.

ततो द्वन्द्वानभिघातः ॥४८॥ tato dvandvānabhighātaḥ ॥48॥

ततः द्वन्द्व–अनभिघातः ।

2.48 Then duality is overcome

Asana helps to overcome the duality. The practice of bodily postures will help to free us from the opposites of raga-dvesha, heat-cold, shocks of sorrows and excitements, etc.

तस्मिन् सति श्वासप्रश्वासयोर्गतिविच्छेदः प्राणायामः ॥४९॥

tasmin sati śvāsapraśvāsayorgativicchedaḥ prāṇāyāmaḥ ॥49॥

तस्मिन् सति श्वास-प्रश्वासयोः गति-विच्छेदः प्राणायामः ।

2.49 After this Pranayama follows, the control of exhalation and inhalation

After having gained proficiency in Asana, the techniques of breath control can be mastered.

Pranayama needs the body to be still and balanced. So Patanjali says that we need to first have mastered a sitting posture like Padmasana or Siddhasana etc. Then only we can start the practice of observing, regulating and modifying the incoming and outgoing breath.

Notice this is how we practice the Sudarshan Kriya, the powerful breathing technique given by Gurudev Sri Sri Ravi Shankar. This is how the slow chant Om Namah Shivaya pranayama is to be done.

बाह्याभ्यन्तरस्तम्भवृत्तिर्देशकालसंख्याभिः परिदृष्टो दीर्घसूक्ष्मः ॥५०॥

(another Reading has this verse as स तु बाह्या...)

bāhyābhyantarastambhavṛttirdeśakālasaṁkhyābhiḥ paridṛṣṭo dīrghasūkṣmaḥ ॥50॥

बाह्य-आभ्यन्तर-स्तम्भ-वृत्तिः देश-काल-संख्याभिः परिदृष्टः दीर्घ-सूक्ष्मः ।

2.50 Regulation of External_Internal_or_Still, governed by Place_Time_and_Count, becomes deep_and_subtle

The three regulations of Pranayama are regulating the patterns of Exhalation, Inhalation and Retention of breath. By taking the Attention to a particular part of the body and varying the Time and Count, the patterns become Long and deep, soft and Subtle.

बाह्याभ्यन्तरविषयाक्षेपी चतुर्थः ॥५१॥

bāhyābhyantaraviṣayākṣepī caturthaḥ ॥51॥

बाह्य–आभ्यन्तर–विषय–आक्षेपी चतुर्थः ।

2.51 Fourth is transcending the Exhalation and Inhalation faculties

The 3 modifications were stated in verse 2.50 of Exhalation, Inhalation and Retention. This verse states a fourth modification that transcends these. It points to the state where the breath has become so subtle that it has merged in the cosmic breath. In other words, Patanjali is saying that the cosmic rhythm is something else and there is the possibility of becoming one with it.

I think that on doing the Sudarshan Kriya, such a state is achieved, atleast it is palpable for most of us in our very 1ˢᵗ Sudarshan Kriya.

ततः क्षीयते प्रकाशावरणम् ॥५२॥ tataḥ kṣīyate prakāśāvaraṇam ॥52॥

ततः क्षीयते प्रकाश–आवरणम् ।

2.52 Then the veil on the Light becomes worn-out

By the practice of Pranayama the veil that covers the Soul gets tattered. Breath Control as learnt from a Master and practiced willingly removes the mask that obscures the Divinity within us.

धारणासु च योग्यता मनसः ॥५३॥ dhāraṇāsu ca yogyatā manasaḥ ॥53॥

धारणासु च योग्यता मनसः ।

2.53 And mind becomes fit for Dharana

Dharana = Focus = Concentration
And the mind gets qualified for Focussing on what is worth.

As long as the noisy thoughts, emotions and memories cloud the Intellect, the mind does not know what path to tread, where to go.

Once Pranayama clears the clouds, the mind can clearly see where to focus.

स्वविषयासम्प्रयोगे चित्तस्य स्वरूपानुकार इवेन्द्रियाणां प्रत्याहारः ॥५४॥
svavisayāsamprayoge cittasya svarūpānukāra ivendriyāṇāṁ pratyāhāraḥ ॥54॥
स्व–विषय–असम्प्रयोगे चित्तस्य स्वरूप–अनुकारः इव इन्द्रियाणां प्रत्याहारः ।

2.54 Pratyahara is like making the Senses follow_the essential_nature_of_the_mind by separating them from their corresponding objects

pratyāhāra = Alternate Food for the Senses = for turning the Senses Inwards = mechanism of Withdrawing the senses

Just like a tortoise withdraws its limbs inside, so in Pratyahara we withdraw the senses inwards, by giving the senses an alternative.

Pratyahara is a mechanism of controlling the outward movement of sense organs like sight, sound, etc. by giving them something inside the body to dwell upon, likewise by dancing and singing, or engaging in any creative fine arts process.

ततः परमा वश्यतेन्द्रियाणाम् ॥५५॥ tataḥ paramā vaśyatendriyāṇām ॥55॥
ततः परमा वश्यता इन्द्रियाणाम् ।

2.55 Thus is Supreme mastery of senses

Pratyahara thus results in total control of the Senses.

॥ ~~~ ॥

Verses that helped me a Lot

1.2 Yoga is living a life whereby one may cool down and slow down the leakages, frustrations, and incessant activities of the Mind

1.12 By the twin disciplines of sustainedEffort and nonEntanglement, the activities can be restrained and tapered off.

1.27 Lord goes by the name of Om, i.e. chanting Om shall help a lot.

1.33 An attitude of friendliness towards the well-off people, compassion towards the downtrodden, delighting and sharing and being happy in the activities of the righteous, and ignoring and shunning the activities and company of the wrongdoers; shall make the mind agreeable and pleasant.

1.34 Or Pranayama e.g. Sudarshan Kriya, can make the mind pleasant and agreeable for living well.

2.1 Enthusiastic Spiritual Practice, Self-Study and Reflection, and being grateful to one's Guru are pointers towards Divinity.

2.10 Kleshas or tendencies are very subtle and need to be faced upfront.

2.11 Meditation will alleviate the Kleshas.

2.30, 2.32 Yama and Niyama give a very big start to the perfect life.

2.39 Apraigraha, being non-greedy is actually easy and highly beneficial.

2.42 Santosha, contentedness though harder, is doable.

What helps You? Jot it down.

विभूतिपादः vibhūtipādaḥ

Mystical Aspects

SANYAM, RESTRAINT and SIDDHI
The Superpowers and Accomplishments

देशबन्धश्चित्तस्य धारणा ॥ १ ॥ deśabandhaścittasya dhāraṇā ॥1॥
देश-बन्धः चित्तस्य धारणा ॥

3.1 Dharana is Fixing the mind at a place

dhāraṇā = *Concentration is holding the mind at a particular place.*
e.g. Bringing the focus to the third-eye is Dharana.
e.g. Concentration on baking the cake is Dharana.

तत्र प्रत्ययैकतानता ध्यानम् ॥ २ ॥ tatra pratyayaikatānatā dhyānam ॥2॥
तत्र प्रत्यय-एकतानता ध्यानम् ॥

3.2 There the unbroken flow of similar thoughts is Dhyana

dhyāna = *Contemplation. Is having a stream of like thoughts towards some topic, object, matter or subject, without consciously trying. Bringing the mind to the present moment.*
e.g. Having prolonged thoughts regarding third-eye, Ajna Chakra, between the eye-brows, etc. is Dhyana.
e.g. Repeatedly having thoughts regarding what to bake for the birthday party is Dhyana.

After a while, when one is not holding the mind, yet it stays, it is called Dhyana or Contemplation.

तदेवार्थमात्रनिर्भासं स्वरूपशून्यमिव समाधिः ॥ ३ ॥

tadevārthamātranirbhāsaṁ svarūpaśūnyamiva samādhiḥ ॥3॥

तदेव अर्थ-मात्र-निर्भासं स्वरूप-शून्यम् इव समाधिः ॥

3.3 Samadhi is illumination of that meaning only, having lost all notion

samādhi = Deep Meditation occurs when the focus has dissolved, thoughts have vanished, personality has evaporated, and only an awareness lingers. Meditation is when the notion of body and mind vanishes and only a faint sensation remains.

त्रयमेकत्र संयमः ॥ ४ ॥ trayamekatra saṁyamaḥ ॥4॥

त्रयम् एकत्र संयमः ॥

3.4 Sanyam is these three together

Sanyam is Dharana, Dhyana, Samadhi in sequence becoming fused.
त्रयम् = trio , एकत्र = all together
When

> *1. Concentration results in a*

> *2. Contemplation, a Flow of similar thoughts and that results in*

> *3. Meditation or Losing self-awareness or Samadhi,*

it is called Sanyam.

Sanyam is a very typical Yogic process that is a type of Restraint of all faculties and thoughts. By Sanyam many Siddhis develop, that make life smooth, successful and aligned to Dharma.

Just as any Yogic practice needs initiation by a Master for it to blossom in life, so also Sanyam needs a Guru to spark it and guide the devotee.

तज्जयात्प्रज्ञालोकः ॥५॥ tajjayātprajñālokaḥ ॥5॥

तत् जयात् प्रज्ञा आलोकः ॥

3.5 By its Mastery emanates the Light of Intelligence

By the Mastery of Sanyam wisdom shines forth.

तस्य भूमिषु विनियोगः ॥६॥ tasya bhūmiṣu viniyogaḥ ॥6॥

तस्य भूमिषु विनियोगः ॥

3.6 Its progress is in degrees

The Mastery of Sanyam takes place gradually in several steps. Its foundation is made by slow and steady progress.

Patanjali says that we need not rush our practice. It will happen by and by.

त्रयमन्तरङ्गं पूर्वेभ्यः ॥७॥ trayamantaraṅgaṁ pūrvebhyaḥ ॥7॥

त्रयम् अन्तरङ्गं पूर्वेभ्यः ॥

3.7 These Three are closer than those mentioned earlier

Earlier in the Sadhana Pada the discussion on the 8 limbs of Yoga was started in verse 2.30 and the five limbs 2.30 Yama, 2.32 Niyama, 2.46 Asana, 2.49 Pranayama 2.54 Pratyahara were stated.

Now the remaining three limbs have been given 3.1 Dharana, 3.2 Dhyan, 3.3 Samadhi, and it is specifically stated that these three limbs are closer to the goal.

तदपि बहिरङ्गं निर्बीजस्य ॥८॥ tadapi bahiraṅgaṁ nirbījasya ॥8॥

तदपि बहिरङ्गं निर्बीजस्य ॥

3.8 Even so, distant from the Seedless State

Dharana, Dhyan and Samadhi are closer to the goal of Yoga but still distant from the state of perfect Enlightenment. Achieving a Yogic state is rare and achieving the highest Yogic state is certainly remote.

In this verse, Patanjali hints that Enlightenment also may have levels. But that is not something to be bothered about.

व्युत्थाननिरोधसंस्कारयोरभिभवप्रादुर्भावौ निरोधक्षणचित्तान्वयो निरोधपरिणामः ॥९॥

vyutthānanirodhasaṁskārayorabhibhavaprādurbhāvau nirodhakṣaṇacittānvayo nirodhapariṇāmaḥ ॥9॥

व्युत्थान–निरोध–संस्कारयोः अभिभव–प्रादुर्भावौ निरोध–क्षण–चित्त–अन्वयः निरोध–परिणामः ॥

3.9 Stages of Control are Giving_way_of_Tendencies, Lessening_of_Moods, Filtering_on_the_Spur_Thoughts

Verse 3.6 stated that Sanyam should proceed gradually in degrees. Here these stages are outlined. The stages are stated in terms of the control that the mind starts to have.

The degrees to which Sanyam is achieved are
- *First the mind starts to shelve its wrong tendencies or improper inclinations*
- *Then the mind drops its mood swings and stubbornness*
- *Finally the mind starts to filter out impromptu thoughts, or momentary thoughts that are irrelevant and not of any use.*

तस्य प्रशान्तवाहिता संस्कारात् ॥१०॥

tasya praśāntavāhitā saṁskārāt ॥10॥

तस्य प्रशान्त–वाहिता संस्कारात् ॥

3.10 Its calmness is attained by habit

Calmness of mind is attained only after many years of practice, when the habit becomes second nature. Only when the Abhyaasa has filtered down to each cell and become a Sanskara does one become Tranquil.

सर्वार्थतैकाग्रतयोः क्षयोदयौ चित्तस्य समाधिपरिणामः ॥११॥

sarvārthataikāgratayoḥ kṣayodayau cittasya samādhipariṇāmaḥ ॥

सर्वार्थता–एकाग्रतयोः क्षय–उदयौ चित्तस्य समाधि–परिणामः ॥

3.11 By Samadhi One-pointedness rises and Agitation tapers

The result of Meditation is that flutteriness tapers and one-pointedness grows.
sarvārthata = Comprehension of several objects = flutteriness
ekāgrata = One-pointedness = intentness on a single subject

ततः पुनः शान्तोदितौ तुल्यप्रत्ययौ चित्तस्यैकाग्रतापरिणामः ॥१२॥

tatah punaḥ śāntoditau tulyapratyayau cittasyaikāgratāpariṇāmaḥ ॥12॥

ततः पुनः शान्त–उदितौ तुल्य–प्रत्ययौ चित्तस्य एकाग्रता–परिणामः ॥

3.12 Then again, by One-pointedness a balance in Peace and Growth results

The result of One-pointedness is that the twin states of the mind viz. calmness and maturity get balanced.

When our thoughts are no longer leaky, when the waviness has waned, then the calmness and the pragmatism, both get nourished. One becomes both Innocent and Intelligent.

एतेन भूतेन्द्रियेषु धर्मलक्षणावस्थापरिणामा व्याख्याताः ॥१३॥

etena bhūtendriyeṣu dharmalakṣaṇāvasthāpariṇāmā vyākhyātāḥ ॥13॥

एतेन भूत–इन्द्रियेषु धर्म–लक्षण–अवस्था–परिणामः व्याख्याताः ॥

**3.13 By this becomes clear the results of Nature_Form_State
In the Elements and Senses**

*One-pointedness results in making Property_Indication_Position
clear. It shows us the behaviour of our Temperament, it shows us
our Personality and also brings to our notice our own Exterior. It
shows the working of the gross elements and also the fine senses.*

dharma = *intrinsic Nature or Temperament*
lakṣaṇa = *Manifest Form i.e. behaviour and personality traits*
avasthā = *State i.e. changing physical or exterior appearance*

*It is the Guru who makes us aware of our basic nature and gives the
solution for the same.*
*It is the parent or a dear friend who criticizes our personality and
what must be done to improve it.*
*It is the colleagues or associates who harp on making adjustments
to our clothes, scents, smartphone and trivia.*

One-pointedness makes it relevant for us.

शान्तोदिताव्यपदेश्यधर्मानुपाती धर्मी ॥ १४ ॥

śāntoditāvyapadeśyadharmānupātī dharmī ॥14॥

शान्त–उदित–अव्यपदेश्य धर्म–अनुपाती धर्मी ॥

**3.14 Dharmi is one who observes Dharma, knowing
Static_Active_Indefinable**

*A righteousness one characterizes conducive acts and knows about
static, active and indefinable traits.*
- dharmī = *Righteous one*
- dharma = *Righteousness = good deeds = conducive acts*
- anupātī = *follows = characterizes*
- śānta = *calm = static*
- udita = *rising up = active*

- avyapadeśya = *indefinable*

क्रमान्यत्वं परिणामान्यत्वे हेतुः ॥ १५ ॥

kramānyatvaṁ pariṇāmānyatve hetuḥ ॥15॥

क्रम–अन्यत्वं परिणाम–अन्यत्वे हेतुः ॥

3.15 Cause of difference in Result is due to difference in Steps

Many times we ask why me? Why it is happening or not happening for me? Patanjali very aptly states the reason. Very simple, he says for the same technique, the methods or procedures are different.

Both of you are doing the Sadhana, yet she is progressing very fast while you are stuck. The reason is she is doing Sadhana after a proper bath and using a good yoga mat. She is also drinking enough water. And doing the Sadhana at a time when there are minimal interruptions, i.e. she has SWITCHED OFF the phone. Whereas you dive into Sadhana straight from bed, the phone is not even in silent mode!

kramānyatvaṁ = *varying steps or differing actions*
pariṇāmānyatve = *difference in Result*

परिणामत्रयसंयमादतीतानागतज्ञानम् ॥ १६ ॥

pariṇāmatrayasaṁyamādatītānāgatajñānam ॥16॥

परिणाम–त्रय–संयमात् अतीत–अनागत–ज्ञानम् ॥

3.16 Sanyam on trio yields Past_Future knowledge

Earlier verse 3.13 specified the trio of dharma_lakshana_avastha i.e. intrinsicNature_manifestForm_changingState

Sanyam on these three will develop the mystical power of knowing about past events and future consequences. Only in relation to us, so that we may thereby steer our ship better.

Many times the mind is so stubborn that it will not budge. It will not take out quality time and effort for Sadhana or Spiritual practices. So a Siddhi is mentioned to hasten a seeker onto the path.

शब्दार्थप्रत्ययानामितरेतराध्यासात् संकरस्तत्प्रविभागसंयमात् सर्वभूतरुतज्ञानम् ॥१७॥

śabdārthapratyayānāmitaretarādhyāsāt saṁkarastatpravibhāgasaṁyamāt sarvabhūtarutajñānam ॥17॥

शब्द–अर्थ–प्रत्ययानाम् इतरेतर अध्यासात् संकरः तत् प्रविभाग–संयमात् सर्व–भूत–रुत–ज्ञानम् ॥

3.17 Mutual imposition of Word_Meaning_Idea gives a soothing mix, by Sanyam on that portion, Speech_of_All_Beings can be understood

Sanyam on an Idea, its Meaning and its Sound mutually imposed suitably will give the Siddhi of being able to understand the speech of animals and birds.

We can decipher the sounds since our faculties get tuned.

संस्कारसाक्षात्करणात् पूर्वजातिज्ञानम् ॥१८॥

saṁskārasākṣātkaraṇāt pūrvajātijñānam ॥18॥

संस्कार–साक्षात् करणात् पूर्व–जाति–ज्ञानम् ॥

3.18 Intuitive_Perception of Latent_Impressions confers knowledge of previous Descents

Sanyam on Sanskaras confers knowledge of the positions held in the past.

प्रत्ययस्य परचित्तज्ञानम् ॥१९॥ pratyayasya paracittajñānam ॥19॥

प्रत्ययस्य पर–चित्त–ज्ञानम् ॥

3.19 By Symbol, a knowledge of Other's Mind

Sanyam on a distinguishing mark confers knowledge of that person's mind. Sanyam on a facial expression, or a birth mark or a body scar will divulge that person's thoughts.

न च तत् सालम्बनं तस्याविषयीभूतत्वात् ॥२०॥

na ca tat sālambanaṁ tasyāviṣayībhūtatvāt ॥20॥

न च तत् सालम्बनं तस्य अविषयी–भूतत्वात् ॥

3.20 But not of his intention since that was not the topic

Sanyam on another person's distinguishing mark confers knowledge of that person's thoughts only, and not of his intentions, since the subject of Sanyam was not to know the intention. A distinguishing mark will simply give an idea of the general psychology, and not of what he is upto. Clarified by Patanjali.

कायरूपसंयमात् तद्ग्राह्यशक्तिस्तम्भे चक्षुःप्रकाशासम्प्रयोगेऽन्तर्धानम् ॥२१॥

kāyarūpasaṁyamāt tadgrāhyaśaktistambhe
cakṣuḥprakāśāsamprayoge'ntardhānam ॥21॥

काय–रूप–संयमात् तत् ग्राह्य–शक्ति–स्तम्भे चक्षुः–प्रकाश–असम्प्रयोगे अन्तर्धानम् ॥

3.21 Sanyam on Body_Form will prevent its visibility, Non-contact of eyes with light causes disappearance

Sanyam on body and its form will supress its visibility just as absence of light to the eyes causes invisibility.

A Yogi who can do Sanyam on body and its form will become invisible since the eyes will no longer perceive any form. We can thus explain some of the tricks that magicians do! They are talented in a particular Sanyam technique.

एतेन शब्दाद्यन्तर्धानमुक्तम् ॥ etena śabdādyantardhānamuktam ॥
एतेन शब्दादि–अन्तर्धानम् उक्तम् ॥

By this the non-hearing of sounds etc. can also be told.

From the text with Bhoja Raja's commentary and Vyasa's Bhashya, this verse is included here. Most commentators agree that it is a part of the Bhashya or gloss and not an aphorism by Patanjali. However in case it is included, then we will have 196 aphorisms by Patanjali instead of 195.

सोपक्रमं निरुपक्रमं च कर्म तत्संयमादपरान्तज्ञानमरिष्टेभ्यो वा ॥२२॥
sopakramaṁ nirupakramaṁ ca karma tatsaṁyamādaparāntajñānamariṣṭebhyo vā ॥22॥
स–उपक्रमं निर्–उपक्रमं च कर्म तत् संयमात् अपरान्त–ज्ञानम् अरिष्टेभ्यः वा ॥

3.22 Sanyam on Soon_Fructified and Late_Fructified Karma gives knowledge regarding separation from body. Or from misfortunes

Karma can be Prarabdha and Sanchita. Sanyam on Prarabdha and Sanchita confers knowledge of time of death.
Or a person with the ability of reading misfortunes can also get such knowledge.

sopakramaṁ = Prarabdha = being frutified now
nirupakramaṁ = Sanchita = will fructify later
aparānta = at separation from body = time of death
ariṣṭa = misfortune or disaster

मैत्र्यादिषु बलानि ॥२३॥ maitryādiṣu balāni ॥23॥
मैत्री–आदिषु बलानि ॥

3.23 On friendliness etc. Strengths develop

*Sanyam on friendliness, compassion, happiness, tenderness,
caring, sharing, etc. confers various Strengths.*
maitrī = *Friendliness, Maitreyee*
maitryādiṣu = *Friendliness etc.*

बलेषु हस्तिबलादीनि ॥२४॥ baleṣu hastibalādīni ॥24॥
बलेषु हस्ति–बल–आदीनि ॥

3.24 On Strength the Strengths of an Elephant etc. manifest

*Sanyam on strength will manifest the strength and qualities of an
elephant. There is an etcetra in this verse, to extrapolate it to
likewise subjects.*
e.g. Sanyam on Courage will manifest virtues of a lion
e.g. Sanyam on Swiftness will manifest virtues of a stallion

प्रवृत्त्यालोकन्यासात् सूक्ष्मव्यवहितविप्रकृष्टज्ञानम् ॥२५॥

pravṛttyālokanyāsat sūkṣmavyavahitaviprakṛṣṭajñānam ॥25॥
प्रवृत्ति–आलोक–न्यासात् सूक्ष्म–व्यवहित–विप्रकृष्ट–ज्ञानम् ॥

3.25 Fixing on Effulgence manifests knowledge of Subtle_Concealed_Obscure

*Sanyam on the luminous Thought manifests knowledge of the
subtle, the hidden and the elusive.*

भुवनज्ञानं सूर्ये संयमात् ॥२६॥ bhuvanajñānaṁ sūrye saṁyamāt ॥26॥
भुवन–ज्ञानं सूर्ये संयमात् ॥

3.26 Sanyam on the Sun manifests knowledge of the worlds

*Sanyam on the luminous Sun manifests knowledge of the fourteen
lokas.*

bhuvan = *chaturdash bhuvanani = fourteen lokas = the layers of
existence consisting of beings of various capabilities*

चन्द्रे ताराव्यूहज्ञानम् ॥२७॥ candre tārāvyūhajñānam ॥27॥

चन्द्रे तारा-व्यूह-ज्ञानम् ॥

3.27 On the Moon develops knowledge of the asterisms

Sanyam on the luminous Moon develops knowledge of the constellations and zodiacs and nakshatras.

ध्रुवे तद्गतिज्ञानम् ॥२८॥ dhruve tadgatijñānam ॥28॥

ध्रुवे तत् गति-ज्ञानम् ॥

3.28 On the Pole-Star fosters knowledge of that movement

Sanyam on the luminous Pole-Star fosters knowledge regarding the planetary motions and the movements of the constellations.

नाभिचक्रे कायव्यूहज्ञानम् ॥२९॥ nābhicakre kāyavyūhajñānam ॥29॥

नाभि-चक्रे काय-व्यूह-ज्ञानम् ॥

3.29 On the Nabhi Chakra comes knowledge of the body constitution

Sanyam on the Navel Center advances knowledge regarding the body structure and makeup.

कण्ठकूपे क्षुत्पिपासानिवृत्तिः ॥३०॥ kaṇṭhakūpe kṣutpipāsānivṛttiḥ ॥30॥

कण्ठ-कूपे क्षुत्-पिपासा-निवृत्तिः ॥

3.30 On the kaṇṭha_kūp fosters cessation of hunger and thirst

Sanyam on the Well of the Throat helps ease pangs of hunger and thirst by stimulating the Vagus nerve. We can go without eating and drinking. Also if the occasion demands, we can eat properly and enjoy all dishes.

kaṇṭha_kūpa = *Deep Throat, WellofThroat, Throat cavity, Throat pit*
kṣut = *hunger,* pipāsā = *thirst,* nivṛttiḥ = *cessation*

A very important technique, since hunger and thirst are primal needs and these desires in turn lead to bigger ones like lust, obsession and frantic-shopping. This Sanyam curbs those as well.

कूर्मनाड्यां स्थैर्यम् ॥३१॥ kūrmanāḍyāṁ sthairyam ॥31॥
कूर्म–नाडचां स्थैर्यम् ॥

3.31 On the kūrma_nādī develops Steadfastness

Sanyam on the Kurma Nadi develops freedom from fears of ups-and-downs. Mind becomes firm. Fickleness vanishes.
Fears give rise to innumerable, far-reaching unwarranted actions and words, so this technique of soothing misgivings assumes great importance.

Traditionally a tortoise is the symbol of stability.

kūrma_nādī = Trachea = tortoise tube = foodpipe = area of chest where hand goes to stabilize oneself or to show sign of fear or discomfort.

मूर्धज्योतिषि सिद्धदर्शनम् ॥३२॥ mūrdhajyotiṣi siddhadarśanam ॥32॥
मूर्ध–ज्योतिषि सिद्ध–दर्शनम् ॥

3.32 On light of Crown gives vision of Siddhas

Sanyam on the Brahmarandhra gives vision of Siddhas.

mūrdhajyotiṣa = Aperture in the Skull = Brahmarandhra
(perhaps it refers to pineal gland or to the central nerve, sushumna)
siddha = perfected being = a Yogi

प्रातिभाद्वा सर्वम् ॥३३॥ prātibhādvā sarvam ॥33॥
प्रातिभात् वा सर्वम् ॥

3.33 Or by Intuition All

Or by intuition all is known.
*Here "Or" can mean by Intuition **alone**.*
*Else "Or" can mean by intuition **everything**.*

prātibha = *Intuition*

हृदये चित्तसंवित् ॥३४॥ hṛdaye cittasaṁvit ॥34॥

हृदये चित्त–संवित् ॥

3.34 On Heart mind is discerned

*By Sanyam on the Heart, mind is divined. The Yogi comes to know
about intentions of his own mind, also of other minds.*

सत्त्वपुरुषयोरत्यन्तासंकीर्णयोः प्रत्ययाविशेषो भोगः परार्थत्वात् स्वार्थसंयमात् पुरुषज्ञानम्
॥३५॥

sattvapuruṣayoratyantāsaṁkīrṇayoh pratyayāviśeso bhogaḥ
parārthatvāt svārthasaṁyamāt puruṣajñānam ॥35॥

सत्त्व–पुरुषयोः अत्यन्त–असंकीर्णयोः प्रत्यय–अविशेषः भोगः पर–अर्थत्वात्
स्वार्थ–संयमात् पुरुष–ज्ञानम् ॥

3.35 By Sanyam on the Experience for the sake_of_the_Seer is gained knowledge of the Soul. A Sattvic Self, a Complete detachment and Unqualified Notions characterize this

*One seeks to enjoy, being unaware of the distinction between the
Seer and the Seen. However by Sanyam on the experience for the
sake of the Seer, is gained the knowledge of the Soul.*

sattva puruṣayo = *of the Sattvic Self = of the Radiant portion*
atyanta asankirnayoḥ = *total unmixing = complete detachment*
pratyaya aviśeṣaḥ = *indistinct notion*
bhogaḥ = *enjoyment = experience*
parārthatvāt = *for the Para = for the higher Self*

ततः प्रातिभश्रावणवेदनादर्शास्वादवार्ता जायन्ते ॥३६॥

tataḥ prātibhaśrāvaṇavedanādarśāsvādavārtā jāyante ॥36॥

ततः प्रातिभ–श्रावण–वेदना–आदर्श–आस्वाद–वार्ताः जायन्ते ॥

3.36 Then is born intuition, divine hearing, divine touch, divine sight, divine taste, divine smell

Continuing from previous verse 3.35, By Sanyam on the experience for the sake of the seer, such divine faculties arise.

ते समाधावुपसर्गा व्युत्थाने सिद्धयः ॥३७॥

te samādhāvupasargā vyutthāne siddhayaḥ ॥37॥

ते समाधौ उपसर्गाः व्युत्थाने सिद्धयः ॥

3.37 Those eclipse immersing in Samadhi by proving to be impediments

From previous verse 3.36, the divine faculties that arise, those Siddhis can be detrimental for Samadhi.

Patanjali introduces an important point by clearly stating that Siddhis are not the goal. They arise during the Sadhana, however one must not get bound by them. Do not get stuck to a Siddhi.

बन्धकारणशैथिल्यात्प्रचारसंवेदनाच्च चित्तस्य परशरीरावेशः ॥३८॥

bandhakāranaśaithilyātpracārasaṁvedanācca cittasya
paraśarīrāveśaḥ ॥38॥

बन्ध–कारण–शैथिल्यात् प्रचार–संवेदनात् च चित्तस्य पर–शरीर–आवेशः ॥

3.38 By letting go of the_cause_of_bondage and the_mind's travel_through_the_organs, another body is entered

When bondage to this body is loosened, and the divine faculties get sharpened, then one can leave this frame and enter another.

This is a Siddhi.

उदानजयाज्जलपङ्ककण्टकादिष्वसङ्ग उत्क्रान्तिश्च ॥३९॥

udānajayājjalapaṅkakaṇṭakādiṣvasaṅga utkrāntiśca ॥39॥

उदान–जयात् जल–पङ्क–कण्टक–आदिषु असङ्गः उत्क्रान्तिः च ॥

3.39 By conquering Udāna, one doesn't sink in water, one can navigate through swamp, one can walk on thorns etc. and rise above such

By mastery over the vital air Udana, one attains such and other similar siddhis, i.e. not sinking in water, navigating a swamp, being untouched by thorns, etc., and one also rises above such petty skills, i.e. one becomes open to new possibilities and faith.

udāna = one of the five vital airs, the prana vayu that is associated with kundalini and upward movement, that expels the soul at the time of death
jayāt = by mastery over
jala_paṅka_kaṇṭaka ādishu = water_swamp_thorn etc.
asaṅga = disassociation = untouched
utkrāntiś ca = and rise above

Note – Ujjayi breath balances Udana vayu. The seat of Udana vayu is the throat and the Vishuddhi Chakra.

समानजयाज्ज्वलनम् ॥४०॥ samānajayājjvalanam ॥40॥

समान–जयात् ज्वलनम् ॥

3.40 By conquering Samāna, one glows

By mastery over the vital air Samana, one begins to glow brightly.

Note - Samana vayu is associated with digestive function, i.e. Jathar Agni, the purifying element. It processes not only food, but also thoughts, sensations and emotions. We have heard the term "Undigested thoughts cause stress". The seat of Samana vayu is the abdomen and the Manipura Chakra.

श्रोत्राकाशयोः सम्बन्धसंयमादिव्यं श्रोत्रम् ॥४१॥

śrotrākāśayoḥ sambandhasaṁyamāddivyaṁ śrotram ॥41॥

श्रोत्र–आकाशयोः सम्बन्ध–संयमात् दिव्यं श्रोत्रम् ॥

3.41 Sanyam on the connection between Ear and Space develops divine hearing

By Sanyam on the association between space and its attribute sound, divine hearing is developed.

E.g. telepathy, soul to soul communication.

कायाकाशयोः सम्बन्धसंयमाल्लघुतूलसमापत्तेश्चाकाशगमनम् ॥४२॥

kāyākāśayoḥ
sambandhasaṁyamāllaghutūlasamāpatteścākāśagamanam ॥42॥

काय–आकाशयोः सम्बन्ध–संयमात् लघु–तूल–समापत्तेः च आकाश–गमनम् ॥

3.42 Sanyam on the connection between Body and Space makes one light as cotton and fosters space travel

By Sanyam on the association between body and space, one becomes light as cotton and can travel through space. Space travel is synonymous to air travel here.

बहिरकल्पिता वृत्तिर्महाविदेहा ततः प्रकाशावरणक्षयः ॥४३॥

bahirakalpitā vṛttirmahāvidehā tataḥ prakāśāvaraṇakṣayaḥ ॥43॥

बहिः अकल्पिता वृत्तिः महा–विदेहा ततः प्रकाश–आवरण–क्षयः ॥

3.43 Genuine thought on_the_outer leads to MahaVideha, then the veil on the soul gets worn out

Genuine impulse on the outer leads to supreme unconditioning, then the curtain of ignorance from the soul drops away

- bahiḥ = *outer*
- akalpitā = *genuine = not imaginary*
- vṛttiḥ = *thought, mental focus*

- mahā-videhā = *great disembodiment, used here in the sense of supreme unconditioning*
- tataḥ = *then*
- prakāśa = *light, used here in the sense of soul or divinity*
- āvaraṇa = *veil, covering*
- kṣayaḥ = *worn out, removed*

स्थूलस्वरूपसूक्ष्मान्वयार्थवत्त्वसंयमाद्भूतजयः ॥४४॥

sthūlasvarūpasūkṣmānvayārthavattvasaṁyamādbhūtajayaḥ ॥44॥

स्थूल–स्वरूप–सूक्ष्म–अन्वय–अर्थवत्त्व–संयमात् भूत–जयः ॥

3.44 Sanyam on the significance of the gross_form in succession to the subtle, gives mastery over the Elements

By Sanyam on the elements in succession from the gross to the fine, mastery over them is attained. Here elements refer to space, air, light, water and earth.

Another interpretation is that by Sanyam on the five attributes of a single element, viz.
- sthūla = *hardness e.g. Oxygen is a gas while Water is a liquid*
- svarūpa = *shape e.g. lattice structure*
- sūkṣmā = *intrinsic e.g. Oxygen is life supporting*
- anvaya = *position in the periodic table e.g. O_2 is sixteenth*
- arthavattva = *property like smell or taste e.g. Oxygen is odourless while Chlorine is pungent*

Mastery of all substances is gained.

ततोऽणिमादिप्रादुर्भावः कायसम्पत्तद्धर्मानभिघातश्च ॥४५॥

tato'ṇimādiprādurbhāvaḥ kāyasampattaddharmānabhighātaśca ॥

ततः अणिमादि–प्रादुर्भावः काय–सम्पत् तत् धर्म–अनभिघातः च ॥

3.45 Then Anima etc. manifest, and bodily excellence and its indestructability

Connecting from verse 3.44, this goes on to state that after mastery over the elements,

- *the siddhis of Anima etc. manifest, and*
- *body becomes healthy and fit, and*
- *bodily traits are maintained*

The great attainments Anima etc. are eight in number, as listed in the traditional vedic texts

अणिमा aṇimā = *shrink to become tiny like an atom*

महिमा mahimā = *expand to become huge*

गरिमा garimā = *become as heavy as can be*

लघिमा laghimā = *become light as air*

प्राप्ति prāpti = *ability to extend till the stars, or reach anywhere*

प्राकाम्य prākāmya = *having anything to heart's content*

ईशित्व īśitva = *dominion over all*

वशित्व vaśitva = *subjugation of natural impulses*

रूपलावण्यबलवज्रसंहननत्वानि कायसम्पत् ॥४६॥

rūpalāvaṇyabalavajrasaṁhananatvāni kāyasampat ॥46॥

रूप–लावण्य–बल–वज्र–संहननत्वानि काय–सम्पत् ॥

3.46 Handsomeness, Charm, Strength, Adamantine Toughness are the bodily excellence

Connecting from verse 3.45, this goes on to describe the bodily excellence. These are the features of a superhuman physique.

ग्रहणस्वरूपास्मितान्वयार्थवत्त्वसंयमादिन्द्रियजयः ॥४७॥

grahaṇasvarūpāsmitānvayārthavattvasaṁyamādindriyajayaḥ ॥47॥

ग्रहण–स्वरूप–अस्मिता–अन्वय–अर्थवत्त्व–संयमात् इन्द्रिय–जयः ॥

3.47 Sanyam on Grasping_Quality_Mineness_Concord_Significance gives mastery over Sense organs

Sanyam on the various properties of the senses, viz.
- *grahaṇa = grasping, holding on to, taking in, experiencing*
- *svarūpa = quality or intrinsic nature*
- *asmitā = Mineness, ego of possession*
- *anvaya = concord or connection*
- *arthavattva = Significance, related to meaning*

Gives a mastery over the sense organs

ततो मनोजवित्वं विकरणभावः प्रधानजयश्च ॥४८॥

tato manojavitvaṁ vikaraṇabhāvaḥ pradhānajayaśca ॥48॥

ततः मनः–जवित्वं विकरण–भावः प्रधान–जयः च ॥

3.48 Then MindSwiftness, FreedomfromSenseOrgans, and conquestOfMaterialNature are achieved

Connecting from verse 3.47, this qualifies the Sanyam related to mastery of senses by adding that swiftness of perception, freedom from sense organs and mastery over materialist nature are also achieved.

tataḥ = *then (by visarga sandhi, visarga has become* ओ, *ततः to* ततो *)*

manojavitvaṁ = *swiftness of perception*

vikaraṇabhāvaḥ = *a feeling of freedom from senses*

pradhānajayaḥ = *conquest of materialist nature, prakriti*

सत्त्वपुरुषान्यताख्यातिमात्रस्य सर्वभावाधिष्ठातृत्वं सर्वज्ञातृत्वं च ॥४९॥

sattvapuruṣānyatākhyātimātrasya sarvabhāvādhiṣṭhātṛtvaṁ sarvajñātṛtvaṁ ca ॥49॥

सत्त्व–पुरुष–अन्यता–ख्याति–मात्रस्य सर्व–भाव–अधिष्ठातृत्वं सर्व–ज्ञातृत्वं च ॥

3.49 Establisment of discrimination between Sattva and Purusha gives Omnipresence and Omniscience

A Sanyam with regards to Sattva as being distinct from Purusha gives Omnipresence and Omniscience.

sattva = purity, a quality of balance of the mind
puruṣa = soul = divinity that is attributeless = beyond mind
anyatā = distinct
khyātimātrasya = by awareness of, establishment

तद्वैराग्यादपि दोषबीजक्षये कैवल्यम् ॥५०॥

tadvairāgyādapi doṣabījakṣaye kaivalyam   ॥50॥

तत् वैराग्यात् अपि दोष–बीज–क्षये कैवल्यम् ॥

3.50 Kaivalyam is when by Vairagya even to this, the faulty_latent_seed has got obliterated

Previous verse 3.49 had established a state of Omnipresence and Omniscience. A detachment even to these, will result in the destruction of all latent seeds, i.e. wipe out impressions altogether. This impression-less state is called Kaivalya.

kaivalyam = the perfect spiritual state, the highest enlightenment

When one attains to the post of Prime Minister, and when one is able to drop the notions and entanglements that come with such a high-office, then one gets qualified to achieve the state of emperor-ship. i.e. only when one gets out of the limited identity of holding the top position in a country, does one qualify for world leadership.

In other words, the ultimate post.

स्थान्युपनिमन्त्रणे सङ्गस्मयाकरणं पुनरनिष्टप्रसङ्गात् ॥५१॥

sthānyupanimantraṇe saṅgasmayākaraṇaṁ punaraniṣṭaprasaṅgāt ॥51॥

स्थानि–उपनिमन्त्रणे सङ्ग–स्मय–अकरणं पुनः अनिष्ट–प्रसङ्गात् ॥

3.51 No need for Pride_of_Association nor wonderment_of_Bigger_Lures, since temptation will be strong to pull one back

Previous verse 3.50 had established a state of Emperorship. Here Patanjali cautions that it will bring many lures and all sorts of temptations. Be wary and do not become enticed, since that will cause a fall.

क्षणतत्क्रमयोः संयमाद्विवेकजं ज्ञानम् ॥५२॥

kṣaṇatatkramayoḥ saṁyamādvivekajaṁ jñānam   ॥52॥

क्षण–तत्–क्रमयोः संयमात् विवेक–जं ज्ञानम् ॥

3.52 Sanyam on a unit of Time_and_its_Progression fosters birth of Viveka

By Sanyam on a second and its progress into minutes gives birth to Viveka.

viveka = awareness, jaṁ *= born of*

In this verse, Viveka is used to mean supreme discrimination or total awareness.

जातिलक्षणदेशैरन्यतानवच्छेदात् तुल्ययोस्ततः प्रतिपत्तिः ॥५३॥

jātilakṣaṇadeśairanyatānavacchedāt tulyayostataḥ pratipattiḥ ॥53॥

जाति–लक्षण–देशैः अन्यता अनवच्छेदात् तुल्ययोः ततः प्रतिपत्तिः ॥

3.53 In comparison, this surely discriminates when even Species_Sign_and_Place fail

Distinction is made by identifying Class, Characeristic, and Place of occurrence for any sample. Where even such an analysis fails to identify, the Awareness produced by the Sanyam stated in previous verse 3.52 will surely work.

तारकं सर्वविषयं सर्वथाविषयमक्रमं चेति विवेकजं ज्ञानम् ॥५४॥

tārakaṁ sarvaviṣayaṁ sarvathāviṣayamakramaṁ ceti vivekajaṁ jñānam ॥54॥

तारकं सर्व–विषयं सर्वथा–विषयम् अक्रमं च इति विवेक–जं ज्ञानम् ॥

3.54 Thus, Knowledge born of Awareness Saves from All_Topics and from every_way_of_each_topic simultaneously

Distinction is made by identifying Class, Characeristic, and Place of
tārakaṁ = *saving, shielding, protecting, liberating*
sarva-viṣayaṁ = *all topics, all subjects, all objects*
sarvathā-viṣayam = *everything regarding any subject or object*
akramaṁ = *simultaneously*
ca = *and*
iti = *thus (by vowel sandhi, च + इति = चेति)*
viveka-jaṁ = *born of Viveka, awareness*
jñānam = *Knowledge*

सत्त्वपुरुषयोः शुद्धिसाम्ये कैवल्यमिति ॥५५॥

sattvapuruṣayoḥ śuddhisāmye kaivalyamiti ॥55॥

सत्त्व–पुरुषयोः शुद्धि–साम्ये कैवल्यम् इति ॥

3.55 When the mind_body_Complex attains Soul-like purity, that is Kaivalya

sattva = *purity aspect, here it means the mind-body of the seeker which has become purified*
puruṣa = *soul, divinity, the innermost being*
śuddhi = *pure*
sāmye = *alike*
kaivalyam = *the perfect spiritual state, the highest enlightenment*

iti = *finally done. Here this word is like the full-stop, the final. Like we say after completing solving a mathematics equation QED.*

Patanjali means that while still alive in body, when the actions, speech and thoughts of the ascetic have become pure as the soul, he has attained the state of perfectness, i.e. enlightenment.

|| ~~~ ||

कैवल्यपादः kaivalyapādaḥ

Liberation Aspects

FREEDOM, AUTONOMY, COSMIC LAWS
The Mind's formulae

जन्मौषधिमन्त्रतपःसमाधिजाः सिद्धयः ॥ १ ॥

janmauṣadhimantratapaḥsamādhijāḥ siddhayaḥ ॥1॥

जन्म–ओषधि–मन्त्र–तपः–समाधि–जाः सिद्धयः ॥

4.1 Siddhis are attained by janma, aushadhi, mantra, tapas, or samadhi

janma = *birth, parentage, genes*
auṣadhi = *medicine, herbs, modern day steroids*
mantra = Guru's word, a sacred sound
tapaḥ = *endurance in sadhana, spiritual discipline, perseverance in pursuit*
samādhi = *meditation, contemplation*
jaḥ = *obtain, give rise to*
siddhayaḥ = *talents, accomplishments, divine gifts, superpowers*

When we see a talented scientist, a sportsman, or a musician, we might wonder as to how they acquired such noble skills? Patanjali gives the answer.

जात्यन्तरपरिणामः प्रकृत्यापूरात् ॥२॥

jātyantarapariṇāmaḥ prakṛtyāpūrāt ॥2॥

जाति–अन्तर–परिणामः प्रकृति–आपूरात् ॥

4.2 Resulting change in Status is due to full support of Nature

jāty = *rank, status, position in society, temperament, ability*
prakṛti = *nature, laws of physics*
āpūrāt = *fulfillment, total support*

Of course one has put in one's efforts, and been steadfast in sadhana, then the actual transformation is the direct result of supportive Natural laws.

Patanjali highlights a very very important point here. He states the obvious fact that is taken for granted and hence missed. Nature or physical law or the higher power that is governing the universe is actually very benevolent. It gives full support to perseverance and patience, that results in tremendous growth and blossoming of an individual. Virtually a transformation, as we read in the stories of Edison, Lincoln, Valmiki, Meerabai and so many greats who have trodden this path.

निमित्तमप्रयोजकं प्रकृतीनां वरणभेदस्तु ततः क्षेत्रिकवत् ॥३॥

nimittamaprayojakaṁ prakṛtīnāṁ varaṇabhedastu tataḥ kṣetrikavat ॥3॥

निमित्तम् अप्रयोजकं प्रकृतीनां वरण–भेदः तु ततः क्षेत्रिकवत् ॥

4.3 But Nature works by selective choice like the gardener, so the reasons might seem aimless

nimittam = *cause, reason*
aprayojakaṁ = *apparent, seemingly aimless*
prakṛtīnāṁ = *of physical nature*
varaṇa = *selective*
bhedaḥ = *contrast, choice*

tu = *but*
tataḥ = *then*
kṣetrikavat = *farmer, gardener*

The intentions of a gardener or the farmer cannot be understood at the shallow level. Why he is cutting some branches or blocking a barrage or not-uprooting some weeds, cannot be easily fathomed.

As Guruji says, "if you are dull, the Guru is brilliant. If you are brilliant, the Guru is irrational. If you are irrational, the Guru is irresistible!"

निर्माणचित्तान्यस्मितामात्रात् ॥४॥ nirmāṇacittānyasmitāmātrāt ॥4॥
निर्माण–चित्तानि अस्मिता–मात्रात् ॥

4.4 Development of Minds is from gradations of Ego
nirmāṇa = development, production
cittāni = the minds, the temperaments, the likes and dislikes
asmitā = the sense of mineness, the ego of identity
mātrāt = by degrees, bit by bit, gradation

The unfathomable laws of Karma are introduced here, by simply stating that over many iterations is the mind formed. After many modes of distillation does the consciousness acquire a body.

See Bhagavad Gita verse 4.17
कर्मणो ह्यापि बोद्धव्यम् , बोद्धव्यं च विकर्मणः ।
अकर्मणश्च बोद्धव्यम् , गहना कर्मणो गतिः ॥ Karmic laws are unfathomable.

प्रवृत्तिभेदे प्रयोजकं चित्तमेकमनेकेषाम् ॥५॥

pravṛttibhede prayojakaṁ cittamekamanekeṣām ॥5॥
प्रवृत्ति–भेदे प्रयोजकं चित्तम् एकम् अनेकेषाम् ॥

4.5 Many Minds, many Methods, only one Producer

pravṛtti-bhede = *natural selection, selective laws*
prayojakaṁ = *composer, agency, promoter*
cittam = *quality of mind, temperament, talent*
ekam = *only one*
anekeṣām = *many*

Though the diversity in creation is manifold, only one Consciousness is the Agency for manifestation of all differences.

Simple to understand from a block-buster movie. There are a score of actors, sets, events, talents and plots. However the director is only one.

तत्र ध्यानजमनाशयम् ॥६॥ tatra dhyānajamanāśayam ॥6॥

तत्र ध्यान–जम् अनाशयम् ॥

4.6 Those born of Meditation are free of expectation

tatra = *there, those*
dhyāna-jam = *born of meditation, result of contemplation*
anāśayam = *free of expectation, desireless, free of sorrow*

Continuing from previous verse 4.5, of the many minds formulated through various methods, the ones made of meditation are the ones that are free of expectation and hence sorrow.

A master stroke by Patanjali that has far reaching ramifications. When we say 'Mother's milk is best', 'home food cannot be surpassed', 'the home team has an advantage', etc. we are actually using this very principle. The principle of meditation or contemplation is the principle that simply means – doing with tender loving care, free of worry, free of performance stress.

कर्माशुक्लाकृष्णं योगिनस्त्रिविधमितरेषाम् ॥७॥

karmāśuklākṛṣṇam yoginastrividhamitareṣām ॥7॥

कर्म–अशुक्ल–अकृष्णं योगिनः त्रिविधम् इतरेषाम् ॥

4.7 An Action is neither_Good nor_Bad for the Yogis, for others it is threefold

karma = *action*
aśukla = *non-white = blame worthy = sinful*
akṛṣṇa = *non-black = praise worthy = virtuous*

Actions do not affect a Yogi, since his actions cannot be labelled. For the common man, actions give threefold results, viz. pleasurable, painful and mixed.

A saint talks and acts out of pure compassion. He lives in non-doership. Karma does not get attached to him.

ततस्तद्विपाकानुगुणानामेवाभिव्यक्तिर्वासनानाम् ॥८॥

tatastadvipākānuguṇānāmevābhivyaktirvāsanānām ॥8॥

ततः तत् विपाक–अनुगुणानाम् एव अभिव्यक्तिः वासनानाम् ॥

4.8 Then due to Vasanas, manifestation of Gunas in accordance with IT only, comes to fruition

tataḥ = *then*
tat = *it (continued from previous verse, IT = Action = Karma)*
vipāka = *fruition, resultant*
anuguṇānām = *as per the virtues and vices*
eva = *only*
abhivyakti = *manifestation (visarga has become repha by sandhi)*
vāsanānām = *of expectations, of latent impressions*

A statement of how a soul takes a body and country. Based on the desires inherent in the soul, the birth happens. The body-mind complex, place of birth, environs and parenthood get decided.

जातिदेशकालव्यवहितानामप्यानन्तर्यं स्मृतिसंस्कारयोरेकरूपत्वात् ॥९॥

jātideśakālavyavahitānāmapyānantaryaṁ
smṛtisaṁskārayorekarūpatvāt ॥9॥

जाति–देश–काल–व्यवहितानाम् अपि आनन्तर्यं स्मृति–संस्कारयोः एक–रूपत्वात् ॥

4.9 Even Actions done in separate body_country_or_timePeriod manifest in a single form due to memory_of_latent impression

jāti = *species, behaving like some animal etc., position, rank*
deśa = *place, country*
kāla = *time period, a previous birth, at any stage of life*
vyavahitānām = *screened from view, distant*
api = *even, also*
ānantaryaṁ = *separated, distinct, not related to*

Many times one is puzzled as to how such and such son got born to me? How come my mother-in-law has that nagging quality? Why I behaved stupidly in that situation? What caused the blunder by a sober person? Or one may also wonder - Why she is getting all the credit?

Patanjali says that it is all due to the working of one's karma or tendency. There are latent impressions and memories in the soul. When a soul takes a new body, various desires and expectations get joined from the sum total of all previous births. The behaviour thus caused is a mixture of that.

तासामनादित्वं चाशिषो नित्यत्वात् ॥१०॥ tāsāmanāditvaṁ cāśiṣo nityatvāt ॥
तासाम् अनादित्वं च आशिषः नित्यत्वात् ॥

4.10 And those are beginningless, desire being everlasting

tāsām = *those, of that memory, behaviour, bodies, from previous verse 4.9*
anāditvaṁ = *beginningless*
ca = *and*

āśiṣa = *desire for pleasure, expectation of joy, wish*
nityatvāt = *always, everlasting*

हेतुफलाश्रयालम्बनैः संगृहीतत्वादेषामभावे तदभावः ॥११॥

hetuphalāśrayālambanaiḥ saṁgṛhītatvādeṣāmabhāve tadabhāvaḥ ॥

हेतु–फल–आश्रय–आलम्बनैः संगृहीतत्वात् एषाम् अभावे तत् अभावः ॥

4.11 Held together by dependency on Cause_Effect_Basis, they disappear when it disappears

Continuing from previous verse 4.10, Those memories and behaviours and latent impressions are supported by the cause and effect relationships. When the cause and effect foundation is vanquished, those memories also vanish.

अतीतानागतं स्वरूपतोऽस्त्यध्वभेदाद्धर्माणाम् ॥१२॥

atītānāgataṁ svarūpato'styadhvabhedāddharmāṇām ॥12॥

अतीत–अनागतं स्वरूपतः अस्ति अध्व–भेदात् धर्माणाम् ॥

4.12 Past_and_Future are as per their own Nature, due to differing phase

atīta = what is past, gone
anāgataṁ = what is yet to come, not gone
svarūpataḥ = own nature
asti = are, exist (Tinganta Verbs तिङन्त are rare in the Yoga Sutras!)
adhva = phase, the quality of seasons
bhedāt = due to difference (by sandhi त् has become द्)
dharmāṇām = of properties, of characteristics

The events of the past and of the future happen as per their differing phases.

e.g. Just as seasons change and our moods change,

e.g. just a simple thing such as a rain forecast changes so many plans and commitments, similarly, the events that occur at different times are influenced by the disparity in circumstance. Having satsang in the open Amphitheatre or in the covered Yagnashala, is so much dependent on the weather. And that in turn changes the tone and subject matter of the Satsang.

ते व्यक्तसूक्ष्मा गुणात्मानः ॥१३॥ te vyaktasūkṣmā guṇātmānaḥ ॥13॥

ते व्यक्त–सूक्ष्माः गुण–आत्मानः ॥

4.13 They manifest_or_remain_potential as per Natural Forces

Whether manifested or potential, they are influenced by the Natural Gunas, viz. Sattva, Rajas and Tamas. These change daily and also seasonally. E.g. 4-6am is Sattva, 6-8am is Rajas, 8-10am is Tamas. Guna Atmana = Inherent Traits = Sattva or Pleasantness, Rajas or Activity, Tamas or Inertia

The events that occur will have the colouring of the characteristics inherent in nature. Nature is a composite of three qualities, and the events will be affected by these qualities, albeit in manifest or potential form.

परिणामैकत्वाद्वस्तुतत्त्वम् ॥१४॥ pariṇāmaikatvādvastutattvam ॥14॥

परिणाम–एकत्वात् वस्तु–तत्त्वम् ॥

4.14 Resulting uniformity is the realized entity

A harmonious mixing of the Sattva, Rajas and Tamas becomes the essential nature of the manifested soul

Even though the natural forces individually are poles apart, their mixing produces a uniformity in the reality of their outcome. What we see when two individuals marry, usually with contrasting tastes and temperaments, yet the child born is a wholesome mix of the genes.

e.g. Brass is an alloy of copper and zinc. Even though copper is reddish brown and zinc is bluish silver, brass is a seamless product with uniform golden colour.

वस्तुसाम्ये चित्तभेदात्तयोर्विभक्तः पन्थाः ॥१५॥

vastusāmye cittabhedāttayorvibhaktaḥ panthāḥ ॥15॥

वस्तु–साम्ये चित्त–भेदात् तयोः विभक्तः पन्थाः ॥

4.15 The same Entity, due to diverse mindsets, is perceived differently

Peoples perspectives are dissimilar.
So many times we come across such a situation. Regarding the same child, the father has a particular theory, while the mother has a different opinion.

Patanjali puts the thought down in clear print so that instead of being frazzled, we can see why two minds have a difference of opinion.

न चैकचित्ततन्त्रं वस्तु तदप्रमाणकं तदा किं स्यात् ॥१६॥

na caikacittatantraṁ vastu tadapramāṇakaṁ tadā kiṁ syāt ॥16॥

न च एक–चित्त–तन्त्रं वस्तु तत् अप्रमाणकं तदा किं स्यात् ? ॥

4.16 Nor does an entity exist solely on the thinking of one mindset. Else what would happen in the absence of that mindset?

tat = that, it (noun, by sandhi तत् has become तद्)

tadā = then, else (adverb)

A single perception is not the basis of any person or object. Perceptions change and are in a continuous flux. Peoples opinions change. So it cannot be that even though someone is perceived in a particular manner, that is the whole truth regarding that person.

Patanjali here lays down the cause for courts, lawyers and judges. He indicates that the essential nature of something cannot be solely dependent on someone's perception or opinion.

तदुपरागापेक्षित्वाच्चित्तस्य वस्तु ज्ञाताज्ञातम् ॥ १७ ॥

taduparāgāpekṣitvāccittasya vastu jñātājñātam ॥17॥

तद् उपराग–अपेक्षित्वात् चित्तस्य वस्तु ज्ञात–अज्ञातम् ॥

4.17 Hence as per the polarity of a mindset, an entity is thereby known or unknown

tad = therefore, hence (adverb)
jñāta = known, conceptualized
ajñātam = unknown, unconceptualized, wrongly known

Hence some of us suffer the fate of being unknown or being misunderstood. E.g. Socrates, Galileo.

सदा ज्ञाताश्चित्तवृत्तयस्तत्प्रभोः पुरुषस्यापरिणामित्वात् ॥ १८ ॥

sadā jñātāścittavṛttayastatprabhoḥ puruṣasyāpariṇāmitvāt ॥18॥

सदा ज्ञाताः चित्त–वृत्तयः तत् प्रभोः पुरुषस्य अपरिणामित्वात् ॥

4.18 Always known are the mind's modulations to the unchanging Self, that being its Lord

tat = that, it (noun)

One's inner conscience is the Lord of the mind. Deep within the heart one will always know the tendencies, workings of the mind.

न तत्स्वाभासं दृश्यत्वात् ॥ १९ ॥ na tatsvābhāsaṁ dṛśyatvāt ॥19॥

न तत् स्व–आभासं दृश्यत्वात् ॥

4.19 It is not self luminous, being an external object

tat = that, it (noun). Refers to Mindset.

One's mindset is the object of one's inner perception. It is external to one's conscience. It reflects the light of the Soul. On its own, the mind is not a conscious entity.

Patanjali states the distinction between the mind and the soul.

एकसमये चोभयानवधारणम् ॥२०॥ ekasamaye cobhayānavadhāraṇam ॥
एक–समये च उभय–अन्–अवधारणम् ॥

4.20 Simultaneously both cannot be comprehended

<u>Grammar Note</u>
च 0 + उभयः m1/1 = चोभयः (vowel Sandhi)

चोभयः + अनवधारणम् = चोभयानवधारणम् (compound word Samasa so visarga drops, and then vowel sandhi)

The mind cannot comprehend two things at the same time. It cannot put its complete focus, even though it may get a partial picture of two things.

Heisenberg's uncertainty principle as stated by Patanjali, to explain how the mind operates.

चित्तान्तरदृश्ये बुद्धिबुद्धेरतिप्रसङ्गः स्मृतिसंकरश्च ॥२१॥

cittāntaradṛśye buddhibuddheratiprasaṅgaḥ smṛtisaṁkaraśca ॥21

चित्त–अन्तर–दृश्ये बुद्धि–बुद्धेः अति–प्रसङ्गः स्मृति–संकरः च ॥

4.21 A split mindset is an intellectual mess, causing over crowding and confusion in the memory

A mind within a mind would trash the intellect, play havoc with the emotions and cause utter confusion.

This verse connects to the previous verses, and emphasizes the distinction between mind and soul.

चितेरप्रतिसंक्रमायास्तदाकारापत्तौ स्वबुद्धिसंवेदनम् ॥२२॥

citerapratisaṃkramāyāstadākārāpattau svabuddhisaṃvedanam ॥

चितेः अप्रतिसंक्रमायाः तत् आकार-आपत्तौ स्व-बुद्धि-संवेदनम् ॥

4.22 Mind assumes its form, and intellect its intelligence, from the unchanging Self

tat = that, it (noun. By sandhi तत् has become तद्)

द्रष्टृदृश्योपरक्तं चित्तं सर्वार्थम् ॥२३॥

draṣṭṛdṛśyoparaktaṃ cittaṃ sarvārtham ॥23॥

द्रष्टृ-दृश्य-उपरक्तं चित्तं सर्वार्थम् ॥

4.23 All the Mind's functioning is by the Seer_Seen context

The mind senses that there is something within i.e. the Seer, and understands all there is without i.e. the Seen.

तदसंख्येयवासनाभिश्चित्रमपि परार्थं संहत्यकारित्वात् ॥२४॥

tadasaṃkhyeyavāsanābhiścitramapi parārtham saṃhatyakāritvāt॥

तत् असंख्येय-वासनाभिः चित्रम् अपि परार्थं संहत्य कारित्वात् ॥

4.24 Stamped with innumerable impressions, it functions now for_Another through association

parārtham = another's sake, sake of the one beyond, the Soul

The mind has so many desires in the form of stored images. Yet it functions for the Soul, being so associated.

विशेषदर्शिन आत्मभावभावनाविनिवृत्तिः ॥२५॥

viśeṣadarśina ātmabhāvabhāvanāvinivṛttiḥ ॥25॥

विशेष-दर्शिनः आत्म-भाव-भावना-विनिवृत्तिः ॥

4.25 Notions cease for the Yogi who sees the Soul and Emotion as distinct

viśeṣa = distinct
darśinaḥ = of a Yogi, of the one who sees beyond
ātmā = Soul
bhāva = emotion, mind stuff, lower tendencies
bhāvanā = notion, imagination
vinivṛttiḥ = ceases

तदा विवेकनिम्नं कैवल्यप्राग्भारं चित्तम् ॥२६॥

tadā vivekanimnaṁ kaivalyaprāgbhāraṁ cittam ॥26॥

तदा विवेक–निम्नं कैवल्य–प्राक्–भारं चित्तम् ॥

4.26 Then the Mind surrenders to Viveka, and gravitates towards Kaivalya

tadā = then
viveka = the discriminative power, the awareness of truth
kaivalya = Enlightenment
prāk = towards
bhāraṁ = deflected, pressurised, gravitates
cittam = mind

Continuing from previous verse 4.25, when the notions regarding emotions or lower tendencies in the mind cease, Then the mind yields to its Awareness attribute, and gets deflected towards Enlightenment.

तच्छिद्रेषु प्रत्ययान्तराणि संस्कारेभ्यः ॥२७॥

tacchidreṣu pratyayāntarāṇi saṁskārebhyaḥ ॥27॥

तत् छिद्रेषु प्रत्यय–अन्तराणि संस्कारेभ्यः ॥

4.27 In the gaps it has offsetting_thoughts based on latent impressions

tat = *it*. chidreṣu = *in the gaps*. pratyaya = *thought*.
antarāṇi = *offsets, others*
saṁskārebhyaḥ = *from latent impressions*

The previous verse 4.26 stated that the mind gets deflected towards enlightenment, as it becomes more and more aware. However in the gaps when it misses the awareness, or between two moments when it holds awareness, other thoughts creep in due to latent impressions.

हानमेषां क्लेशवदुक्तम् ॥२८॥ hānameṣāṁ kleśavaduktam ॥28॥
हानम् एषां क्लेशवत् उक्तम् ॥

4.28 Their eradication is as said before, regarding klesha

Ways to avoid the thoughts that creep in, ways to maintain the awareness, have been enumerated before. Just as ways to eradicate the afflictions have been stated earlier in Sadhana Pada and Vibhooti Pada, by means of the Eight Limbs of Yoga. Mainly the Meditative practices and Sanyam.

प्रसंख्यानेऽप्यकुसीदस्य सर्वथा विवेकख्यातेर्धर्ममेघः समाधिः ॥२९॥
prasaṁkhyāne'pyakusīdasya sarvathā
vivekakhyāterdharmameghaḥ samādhiḥ ॥29॥
प्रसंख्याने अपि अकुसीदस्य सर्वथा विवेक–ख्यातेः धर्म–मेघः समाधिः ॥

4.29 After Awareness gets established, only if no interest is shown towards attaining anything lofty, the Dharma Megha Samadhi happens

prasaṁkhyāne = in lofty attainments
api = only when
akusīdasya = disinterest, dispassion
sarvathā = anything, everything
viveka = awareness
khyāteḥ = established in
dharma-meghaḥ = cloud of Dharma = space of pure consciousness
samādhiḥ = Samadhi = deep meditation

Patanjali says that to hold on the peak, to maintain the state of enlightenment, any and all inclinations have to be shelved completely. Such a state is called being in the space of pure consciousness.

Patanjali has perfected the Art of Teaching. He leaves nothing to chance. For the aspirant who has scaled the highest peak, he offers the technique of holding it there. He gives the advice of maintaining the PLATEAU ON THE PEAK.

ततः क्लेशकर्मनिवृत्तिः ॥३०॥ tataḥ kleśakarmanivṛttiḥ ॥30॥
ततः क्लेश–कर्म–निवृत्तिः ॥

4.30 Then is freedom from Klesha and Karma

tataḥ = then
kleśa = affliction, any tendency that is painful
karma = Action that produces latent impression, action that leaves an imprint
nivṛttiḥ = freedom, cessation, full stop

Being in the space of pure consciousness is being free. Such a state is the state of the Lord. It is an inner state, not a flavour or attribute of the body-mind complex. It cannot be known nor divined. Only the one who has it knows it, but it cannot be noticed by anyone else.

तदा सर्वावरणमलापेतस्य ज्ञानस्यानन्त्याज्ज्ञेयमल्पम् ॥३१॥

tadā sarvāvaraṇamalāpetasya jñānasyānantyājjñeyamalpam ॥31॥
तदा सर्व–आवरण–मल–अपेतस्य ज्ञानस्य आनन्त्यात् ज्ञेयम् अल्पम् ॥

4.31 Then devoid of all covering and impurity, the wisdom becomes vast, the unknown becomes insignificant

tadā = then. sarv = all. āvaraṇa = veil, covering, dust
mala = impurity, stain. apetasya = gone, cleared
jñānasya = of knowledge, wisdom. ānantyāt = from limitless, vast

jñeyam = something yet to be known, the unknown
alpam= insignificant, little

For the one who is in the space of Dharma Megha Samadhi, the wisdom is infinite, the unknown non-existent.

तत: कृतार्थानां परिणामक्रमसमाप्तिर्गुणानाम् ॥३२॥

tataḥ kṛtārthānāṁ pariṇāmakramasamāptirguṇānām ॥32॥

तत: कृत–अर्थानां परिणाम–क्रम–समाप्ति: गुणानाम् ॥

4.32 Thereafter comes the ending of the Gunas and results of their iterations, their purpose being done

tataḥ = then, thereafter. kṛtārthānāṁ = purpose being done
pariṇāma = result. krama = iteration

samāptiḥ = THE END.

guṇānām = of the Gunas, of the Sattva, Rajas and Tamas

The MIGHTY PRAKRITI, *with its threefold gunas, comes to a full stop for the one established in Dharma Megha Samadhi.*

Let us reflect a bit and understand this better. We all like to sleep well, and we all like to get up fresh. Then we all exit this body and take on another. This is a sort of birth and death, this is a kind of cycle. <u>But this is NOT the cycle of Samsara that is the crux of the matter in spirituality.</u>

Q. In Yoga, on the Divine path, what is the final teaching? What is the full stop or End?
A. It is the skill in handling wounds, bitterness, guilt, blame and fear. It is the state where such events and emotions become fleeting. It is the state when feverishness doesn't last more than a few moments. Samsara refers to that alone, not to sleep-and-waking, not to physical-death-and-birth. **Samāptiḥ** The END refers to the Ending of such Thoughts.

क्षणप्रतियोगी परिणामापरान्तनिर्ग्राह्यः क्रमः ॥३३॥

kṣaṇapratiyogī pariṇāmāparāntanirgrāhyaḥ kramaḥ ॥33॥

क्षण–प्रतियोगी परिणाम–अपरान्त–निर्ग्राह्यः क्रमः ॥

4.33 Understanding the Sequence of successive_moments results in the finality

- kṣaṇa = moment
- pratiyogī = counterpart, succession
- pariṇāma = change, resultant
- aparānta = other end, finality
- nirgrāhyaḥ = grasping, holding, understanding
- kramaḥ = sequence

The one who has understood TIME, *by the progression of its each second, he reaches the* END *where time* STANDS STILL.

पुरुषार्थशून्यानां गुणानां प्रतिप्रसवः कैवल्यं स्वरूपप्रतिष्ठा वा चितिशक्तिरिति ॥३४॥

purusārthaśūnyānāṁ gunānāṁ pratiprasavaḥ kaivalyaṁ svarūpapratiṣṭhā vā citiśaktiriti ॥34॥

पुरुषार्थ–शून्यानां गुणानां प्रतिप्रसवः कैवल्यं स्वरूप–प्रतिष्ठा वा चिति–शक्तिः इति ॥

4.34 Kaivalyam is being established in the Center, when no more Aims exist, when Gunas are reabsorbed; or the Power of Consciousness

Patanjali sums up

Liberation as Living in the Center,
where no aims exist, when the Gunas are reabsorbed.
Or
Liberation means the power of the Divine, i.e. Grace of the Divine.

puruṣārtha = Dharma Artha Kama Moksha are the fourfold Aims
śūnyānāṁ = of zero, of no more aim
guṇānāṁ = of Gunas, Sattva Rajas Tamas
pratiprasavaḥ = back to the center, re-absorption
kaivalyaṁ = LIBERATION
svarūpa-pratiṣṭhā = standing in its own nature, being at the center
vā = otherwise
citiśaktiḥ = power of consciousness
iti = STOP. (traditionally in the scriptures, 'iti' when it is the last
word, means END of the TEXT.

STOP ‖ ~~~ ‖ SUTRAS END

	1	**अथ पातञ्जलयोगसूत्राणि ॥ अथ समाधिपादः प्रथमः ॥**
1	1.1	अथ योगानुशासनम् ॥
2	1.2	योगश्चित्तवृत्तिनिरोधः ॥
3	1.3	तदा द्रष्टुः स्वरूपेऽवस्थानम् ॥
4	1.4	वृत्तिसारूप्यमितरत्र ॥
5	1.5	वृत्तयः पञ्चतय्यः क्लिष्टाक्लिष्टाः ॥
6	1.6	प्रमाणविपर्ययविकल्पनिद्रास्मृतयः ॥
7	1.7	प्रत्यक्षानुमानागमाः प्रमाणानि ॥
8	1.8	विपर्ययो मिथ्याज्ञानमतद्रूपप्रतिष्ठम् ॥
9	1.9	शब्दज्ञानानुपाती वस्तुशून्यो विकल्पः ॥
10	1.10	अभावप्रत्ययालम्बना वृत्तिर्निद्रा ॥
11	1.11	अनुभूतविषयासंप्रमोषः स्मृतिः ॥
12	1.12	अभ्यासवैराग्याभ्यां तन्निरोधः ॥
13	1.13	तत्र स्थितौ यत्नोऽभ्यासः ॥
14	1.14	स तु दीर्घकालनैरन्तर्यसत्कारासेवितो दृढभूमिः ॥
15	1.15	दृष्टानुश्रविकविषयवितृष्णस्य वशीकारसंज्ञा वैराग्यम् ॥
16	1.16	तत्परं पुरुषख्यातेर्गुणवैतृष्ण्यम् ॥
17	1.17	वितर्कविचारानन्दास्मितारूपानुगमात् संप्रज्ञातः ॥
18	1.18	विरामप्रत्ययाभ्यासपूर्वः संस्कारशेषोऽन्यः ॥
19	1.19	भवप्रत्ययो विदेहप्रकृतिलयानाम् ॥
20	1.20	श्रद्धावीर्यस्मृतिसमाधिप्रज्ञापूर्वक इतरेषाम् ॥
21	1.21	तीव्रसंवेगानामासन्नः ॥
22	1.22	मृदुमध्याधिमात्रत्वात् ततोऽपि विशेषः ॥
23	1.23	ईश्वरप्रणिधानाद्वा ॥
24	1.24	क्लेशकर्मविपाकाशयैरपरामृष्टः पुरुषविशेष ईश्वरः ॥

25   1.25   तत्र निरतिशयं सर्वज्ञबीजम् ॥

26   1.26   पूर्वेषाम् अपि गुरुः कालेनानवच्छेदात् ॥

27   1.27   तस्य वाचकः प्रणवः ॥

28   1.28   तज्जपस्तदर्थभावनम् ॥

29   1.29   ततः प्रत्यक्चेतनाधिगमोऽप्यन्तरायाभावश्च ॥

30   1.30   व्याधिस्त्यानसंशयप्रमादालस्याविरति-
भ्रान्तिदर्शनालब्धभूमिकत्वानवस्थितत्वानि चित्तविक्षेपास्तेऽन्तरायाः ॥

31   1.31   दुःखदौर्मनस्याङ्गमेजयत्वश्वासप्रश्वासा विक्षेपसहभुवः ॥

32   1.32   तत्प्रतिषेधार्थमेकतत्त्वाभ्यासः ॥

33   1.33   मैत्रीकरुणामुदितोपेक्षाणां सुखदुःखपुण्यापुण्यविषयाणां भावनातश्चित्तप्रसादनम् ॥

34   1.34   प्रच्छर्दनविधारणाभ्यां वा प्राणस्य ॥

35   1.35   विषयवती वा प्रवृत्तिरुत्पन्ना मनसः स्थितिनिबन्धिनी ॥

36   1.36   विशोका वा ज्योतिष्मती ॥

37   1.37   वीतरागविषयं वा चित्तम् ॥

38   1.38   स्वप्ननिद्राज्ञानालम्बनं वा ॥

39   1.39   यथाभिमतध्यानाद्वा ॥

40   1.40   परमाणुपरममहत्त्वान्तोऽस्य वशीकारः ॥

41   1.41   क्षीणवृत्तेरभिजातस्येव मणेर्ग्रहीतृग्रहणग्राह्येषु तत्स्थतदञ्जनतासमापत्तिः ॥

42   1.42   तत्र शब्दार्थज्ञानविकल्पैः संकीर्णा सवितर्का समापत्तिः ॥

43   1.43   स्मृतिपरिशुद्धौ स्वरूपशून्येवार्थमात्रनिर्भासा निर्वितर्का ॥

44   1.44   एतयैव सविचारा निर्विचारा च सूक्ष्मविषया व्याख्याता ॥

45   1.45   सूक्ष्मविषयत्वं चालिङ्गपर्यवसानम् ॥

46   1.46   ता एव सबीजः समाधिः ॥

47   1.47   निर्विचारवैशारद्येऽध्यात्मप्रसादः ॥

48   1.48   ऋतम्भरा तत्र प्रज्ञा ॥

49   1.49   श्रुतानुमानप्रज्ञाभ्यामन्यविषया विशेषार्थत्वात् ॥

50	1.50	तज्जः संस्कारोऽन्यसंस्कारप्रतिबन्धी ॥
51	1.51	तस्यापि निरोधे सर्वनिरोधान्निर्बीजः समाधिः ॥ **इति पातञ्जले योगशास्त्रे समाधिपादः ॥**
	2	**अथ साधनपादः द्वितीयः ॥**
52	2.1	तपःस्वाध्यायेश्वरप्रणिधानानि क्रियायोगः ॥
53	2.2	समाधिभावनार्थः क्लेशतनूकरणार्थश्च ॥
54	2.3	अविद्यास्मितारागद्वेषाभिनिवेशाः क्लेशाः ॥
55	2.4	अविद्याक्षेत्रमुत्तरेषां प्रसुप्ततनुविच्छिन्नोदाराणाम् ॥
56	2.5	अनित्याशुचिदुःखानात्मसु नित्यशुचिसुखात्मख्यातिरविद्या ॥
57	2.6	दृग्दर्शनशक्त्योरेकात्मतेवास्मिता ॥
58	2.7	सुखानुशायी रागः ॥
59	2.8	दुःखानुशायी द्वेषः ॥
60	2.9	स्वरसवाही विदुषोऽपि तथारूढो भिनिवेशः ॥
61	2.10	ते प्रतिप्रसवहेयाः सूक्ष्माः ॥
62	2.11	ध्यानहेयास्तद्वृत्तयः ॥
63	2.12	क्लेशमूलः कर्माशयो दृष्टादृष्टजन्मवेदनीयः ॥
64	2.13	सति मूले तद्विपाको जात्यायुर्भोगाः ॥
65	2.14	ते ह्लादपरितापफलाः पुण्यापुण्यहेतुत्वात् ॥
66	2.15	परिणामतापसंस्कारदुःखैर्गुणवृत्तिविरोधाच्च दुःखमेव सर्वं विवेकिनः ॥
67	2.16	हेयं दुःखमनागतम् ॥
68	2.17	द्रष्टृदृश्ययोः संयोगो हेयहेतुः ॥
69	2.18	प्रकाशक्रियास्थितिशीलं भूतेन्द्रियात्मकं भोगापवर्गार्थं दृश्यम् ॥
70	2.19	विशेषाविशेषलिङ्गमात्रालिङ्गानि गुणपर्वाणि ॥
71	2.20	द्रष्टा दृशिमात्रः शुद्धोऽपि प्रत्ययानुपश्यः ॥
72	2.21	तदर्थ एव दृश्यस्यात्मा ॥
73	2.22	कृतार्थं प्रति नष्टमप्यनष्टं तदन्यसाधारणत्वात् ॥

74	2.23	स्वस्वामिशक्त्योः स्वरूपोपलब्धिहेतुः संयोगः ॥
75	2.24	तस्य हेतुरविद्या ॥
76	2.25	तदभावात् संयोगाभावो हानं तद् दृशेः कैवल्यम् ॥
77	2.26	विवेकख्यातिरविप्लवा हानोपायः ॥
78	2.27	तस्य सप्तधा प्रान्तभूमिः प्रज्ञा ॥
79	2.28	योगाङ्गाऽनुष्ठानादशुद्धिक्षये ज्ञानदीप्तिराविवेकख्यातेः ॥
80	2.29	यमनियमासनप्राणायामप्रत्याहारधारणाध्यानसमाधयोऽष्टावङ्गानि ॥
81	2.30	अहिंसासत्यास्तेयब्रह्मचर्यापरिग्रहा यमाः ॥
82	2.31	जातिदेशकालसमयानवच्छिन्नाः सार्वभौमा महाव्रतम् ॥
83	2.32	शौचसंतोषतपःस्वाध्यायेश्वरप्रणिधानानि नियमाः ॥
84	2.33	वितर्कबाधने प्रतिपक्षभावनम् ॥
85	2.34	वितर्का हिंसादयः कृतकारितानुमोदिता लोभक्रोधमोहपूर्वका मृदुमध्याधिमात्रा दुःखाज्ञानानन्तफला इति प्रतिपक्षभावनम् ॥
86	2.35	अहिंसाप्रतिष्ठायां तत्सन्निधौ वैरत्यागः ॥
87	2.36	सत्यप्रतिष्ठायां क्रियाफलाश्रयत्वम् ॥
88	2.37	अस्तेयप्रतिष्ठायां सर्वरत्नोपस्थानम् ॥
89	2.38	ब्रह्मचर्यप्रतिष्ठायां वीर्यलाभः ॥
90	2.39	अपरिग्रहस्थैर्ये जन्मकथंतासंबोधः ॥
91	2.40	शौचात् स्वाङ्गजुगुप्सा परैरसंसर्गः ॥
92	2.41	सत्त्वशुद्धिसौमनस्यैकाग्र्येन्द्रियजयात्मदर्शनयोग्यत्वानि च ॥
93	2.42	संतोषादनुत्तमसुखलाभः ॥
94	2.43	कायेन्द्रियसिद्धिरशुद्धिक्षयात्तपसः ॥
95	2.44	स्वाध्यायादिष्टदेवतासंप्रयोगः ॥
96	2.45	समाधिसिद्धिरीश्वरप्रणिधानात् ॥
97	2.46	स्थिरसुखमासनम् ॥
98	2.47	प्रयत्नशैथिल्यानन्त्यसमापत्तिभ्याम् ॥

99   2.48   ततो द्वन्द्वानभिघातः ॥

100   2.49   तस्मिन् सति श्वासप्रश्वासयोर्गतिविच्छेदः प्राणायामः ॥

101   2.50   बाह्याभ्यन्तरस्तम्भवृत्तिर्देशकालसंख्याभिः परिदृष्टो दीर्घसूक्ष्मः ॥

102   2.51   बाह्याभ्यन्तरविषयाक्षेपी चतुर्थः ॥

103   2.52   ततः क्षीयते प्रकाशावरणम् ॥

104   2.53   धारणासु च योग्यता मनसः ॥

105   2.54   स्वविषयासंप्रयोगे चित्तस्य स्वरूपानुकार इवेन्द्रियाणां प्रत्याहारः ॥

106   2.55   ततः परमा वश्यतेन्द्रियाणाम् ॥ **इति पातञ्जले योगशास्त्रे साधनपादः ॥**

       3   **अथ विभूतिपादः तृतीयः ॥**

107   3.1   देशबन्धश्चित्तस्य धारणा ॥

108   3.2   तत्र प्रत्ययैकतानता ध्यानम् ॥

109   3.3   तदेवार्थमात्रनिर्भासं स्वरूपशून्यमिव समाधिः ॥

110   3.4   त्रयमेकत्र संयमः ॥

111   3.5   तज्जयात्प्रज्ञालोकः ॥

112   3.6   तस्य भूमिषु विनियोगः ॥

113   3.7   त्रयमन्तरङ्गं पूर्वेभ्यः ॥

114   3.8   तदपि बहिरङ्गं निर्बीजस्य ॥

115   3.9   व्युत्थाननिरोधसंस्कारयोरभिभवप्रादुर्भावौ निरोधक्षणचित्तान्वयो निरोधपरिणामः ॥

116   3.10   तस्य प्रशान्तवाहिता संस्कारात् ॥

117   3.11   सर्वार्थतैकाग्रतयोः क्षयोदयौ चित्तस्य समाधिपरिणामः ॥

118   3.12   ततः पुनः शान्तोदितौ तुल्यप्रत्ययौ चित्तस्यैकाग्रतापरिणामः ॥

119   3.13   एतेन भूतेन्द्रियेषु धर्मलक्षणावस्थापरिणामा व्याख्याताः ॥

120   3.14   शान्तोदिताव्यपदेश्यधर्मानुपाती धर्मी ॥

121   3.15   क्रमान्यत्वं परिणामान्यत्वे हेतुः ॥

122   3.16   परिणामत्रयसंयमादतीतानागतज्ञानम् ॥

123   3.17   शब्दार्थप्रत्ययानामितरेतराध्यासात् संकरस्तत्प्रविभागसंयमात् सर्वभूतरुतज्ञानम् ॥

124   3.18   संस्कारसाक्षात्करणात् पूर्वजातिज्ञानम् ॥

125   3.19   प्रत्ययस्य परचित्तज्ञानम् ॥

126   3.20   न च तत् सालम्बनं तस्याविषयीभूतत्वात् ॥

127   3.21   कायरूपसंयमात् तद्ग्राह्यशक्तिस्तम्भे चक्षुःप्रकाशासंप्रयोगेऽन्तर्धानम् ॥

128   3.22   सोपक्रमं निरुपक्रमं च कर्म तत्संयमादपरान्तज्ञानमरिष्टेभ्यो वा ॥

129   3.23   मैत्र्यादिषु बलानि ॥

130   3.24   बलेषु हस्तिबलादीनि ॥

131   3.25   प्रवृत्त्यालोकन्यासात् सूक्ष्मव्यवहितविप्रकृष्टज्ञानम् ॥

132   3.26   भुवनज्ञानं सूर्ये संयमात् ॥

133   3.27   चन्द्रे ताराव्यूहज्ञानम् ॥

134   3.28   ध्रुवे तद्गतिज्ञानम् ॥

135   3.29   नाभिचक्रे कायव्यूहज्ञानम् ॥

136   3.30   कण्ठकूपे क्षुत्पिपासानिवृत्तिः ॥

137   3.31   कूर्मनाड्यां स्थैर्यम् ॥

138   3.32   मूर्धज्योतिषि सिद्धदर्शनम् ॥

139   3.33   प्रातिभाद्वा सर्वम् ॥

140   3.34   हृदये चित्तसंवित् ॥

141   3.35   सत्त्वपुरुषयोरत्यन्तासंकीर्णयोः प्रत्ययाविशेषो भोगः परार्थत्वात् स्वार्थसंयमात् पुरुषज्ञानम् ॥

142   3.36   ततः प्रातिभश्रावणवेदनादर्शास्वादवार्ता जायन्ते ॥

143   3.37   ते समाधावुपसर्गा व्युत्थाने सिद्धयः ॥

144   3.38   बन्धकारणशैथिल्यात्प्रचारसंवेदनाच्च चित्तस्य परशरीरावेशः ॥

145   3.39   उदानजयाज्जलपङ्ककण्टकादिष्वसङ्ग उत्क्रान्तिश्च ॥

146   3.40   समानजयाज्ज्वलनम् ॥

147   3.41   श्रोत्राकाशयोः संबन्धसंयमादिव्यं श्रोत्रम् ॥

148	3.42	कायाकाशयोः संबन्धसंयमाल्लघुतूलसमापत्तेश्चाकाशगमनम् ॥
149	3.43	बहिरकल्पिता वृत्तिर्महाविदेहा ततः प्रकाशावरणक्षयः ॥
150	3.44	स्थूलस्वरूपसूक्ष्मान्वयार्थवत्त्वसंयमाद्भूतजयः ॥
151	3.45	ततोऽणिमादिप्रादुर्भावः कायसंपत्तद्धर्मानभिघातश्च ॥
152	3.46	रूपलावण्यबलवज्रसंहननत्वानि कायसंपत् ॥
153	3.47	ग्रहणस्वरूपास्मितान्वयार्थवत्त्वसंयमादिन्द्रियजयः ॥
154	3.48	ततो मनोजवित्वं विकरणभावः प्रधानजयश्च ॥
155	3.49	सत्त्वपुरुषान्यताख्यातिमात्रस्य सर्वभावाधिष्ठातृत्वं सर्वज्ञातृत्वं च ॥
156	3.50	तद्वैराग्यादपि दोषबीजक्षये कैवल्यम् ॥
157	3.51	स्थान्युपनिमन्त्रणे सङ्गस्मयाकरणं पुनरनिष्टप्रसङ्गात् ॥
158	3.52	क्षणतत्क्रमयोः संयमाद्विवेकजं ज्ञानम् ॥
159	3.53	जातिलक्षणदेशैरन्यतानवच्छेदात् तुल्ययोस्ततः प्रतिपत्तिः ॥
160	3.54	तारकं सर्वविषयं सर्वथाविषयमक्रमं चेति विवेकजं ज्ञानम् ॥
161	3.55	सत्त्वपुरुषयोः शुद्धिसाम्ये कैवल्यमिति ॥ **इति पातञ्जले योगशास्त्रे विभूतिपादः ॥**
	4	**अथ कैवल्यपादः चतुर्थः ॥**
162	4.1	जन्मौषधिमन्त्रतपःसमाधिजाः सिद्धयः ॥
163	4.2	जात्यन्तरपरिणामः प्रकृत्यापूरात् ॥
164	4.3	निमित्तमप्रयोजकं प्रकृतीनां वरणभेदस्तु ततः क्षेत्रिकवत् ॥
165	4.4	निर्माणचित्तान्यस्मितामात्रात् ॥
166	4.5	प्रवृत्तिभेदे प्रयोजकं चित्तमेकमनेकेषाम् ॥
167	4.6	तत्र ध्यानजमनाशयम् ॥
168	4.7	कर्माशुक्लाकृष्णं योगिनस्त्रिविधमितरेषाम् ॥
169	4.8	ततस्तद्विपाकानुगुणानामेवाभिव्यक्तिर्वासनानाम् ॥
170	4.9	जातिदेशकालव्यवहितानामप्यानन्तर्यं स्मृतिसंस्कारयोरेकरूपत्वात् ॥
171	4.10	तासामनादित्वं चाशिषो नित्यत्वात् ॥

172   4.11   हेतुफलाश्रयालम्बनैः संगृहीतत्वादेषामभावे तदभावः ॥

173   4.12   अतीतानागतं स्वरूपतोऽस्त्यध्वभेदाद्धर्माणाम् ॥

174   4.13   ते व्यक्तसूक्ष्मा गुणात्मानः ॥

175   4.14   परिणामैकत्वाद्वस्तुतत्त्वम् ॥

176   4.15   वस्तुसाम्ये चित्तभेदात्तयोर्विभक्तः पन्थाः ॥

177   4.16   न चैकचित्ततन्त्रं वस्तु तदप्रमाणकं तदा किं स्यात् ॥

178   4.17   तदुपरागापेक्षित्वाचित्तस्य वस्तु ज्ञाताज्ञातम् ॥

179   4.18   सदा ज्ञाताश्चित्तवृत्तयस्तत्प्रभोः पुरुषस्यापरिणामित्वात् ॥

180   4.19   न तत्स्वाभासं दृश्यत्वात् ॥

181   4.20   एकसमये चोभयानवधारणम् ॥

182   4.21   चित्तान्तरदृश्ये बुद्धिबुद्धेरतिप्रसङ्गः स्मृतिसंकरश्च ॥

183   4.22   चितेरप्रतिसंक्रमायास्तदाकारापत्तौ स्वबुद्धिसंवेदनम् ॥

184   4.23   द्रष्टृदृश्योपरक्तं चित्तं सर्वार्थम् ॥

185   4.24   तदसंख्येयवासनाभिश्चित्रमपि परार्थं संहत्यकारित्वात् ॥

186   4.25   विशेषदर्शिन आत्मभावभावनाविनिवृत्तिः ॥

187   4.26   तदा विवेकनिम्नं कैवल्यप्राग्भारं चित्तम् ॥

188   4.27   तच्छिद्रेषु प्रत्ययान्तराणि संस्कारेभ्यः ॥

189   4.28   हानमेषां क्लेशवदुक्तम् ॥

190   4.29   प्रसंख्यानेऽप्यकुसीदस्य सर्वथा विवेकख्यातेर्धर्ममेघः समाधिः ॥

191   4.30   ततः क्लेशकर्मनिवृत्तिः ॥

192   4.31   तदा सर्वावरणमलापेतस्य ज्ञानस्यानन्त्याज्ज्ञेयमल्पम् ॥

193   4.32   ततः कृतार्थानां परिणामक्रमसमाप्तिर्गुणानाम् ॥

194   4.33   क्षणप्रतियोगी परिणामापरान्तनिर्ग्राह्यः क्रमः ॥

195   4.34   पुरुषार्थशून्यानां गुणानां प्रतिप्रसवः कैवल्यं स्वरूपप्रतिष्ठा वा चितिशक्तिरिति ॥

इति पातञ्जले योगशास्त्रे विभूतिपादः ॥ समाप्तमिदं पातञ्जलयोगदर्शनं ॥

Sanskrit Word Index

The word index gives the Sutra and the Word. Many long words are Compounds or else joined due to Sandhi. **Ending letter is left as such for ease in locating**. Some words have Visarga Dropped due to Sandhi. A final मकार changes to Anusvara, however not when facing a vowel.

<u>Grammar Notes</u>

The stem तद् [mfn] declines when used as a Pronoun in 1st case as

सः [m1/1] He , सा [f1/1] She , तत् [n1/1] It , तत् [n2/1] That/This

By जश्त्व Sandhi, spelling of तत् changes to तद् । When used in a compound, stem तद् takes the form तत् as prior member.

When तद् is used as an Adverb, it is an indeclinable. (ततः [0] = Hence/Due to) तद् [0] Thus/Therefore. Such an occurrence is noticed only in Sutra 4.17, at all other places it is the pronoun तत् । When used as a pronoun, the meaning in English will variously become singular or plural, to fully express the content of a Verse.

Since Sanskrit is an inflectional language, the **spelling of the same word** changes as per context or usage. This matrix shows how.							
Masculine stem vowel अ ending			Masculine stem consonant त् ending				
राम [m] Lord's name			मरुत् [m] Wind, Breeze, Air				
	single [1]	dual [2]	plural [3]	Usage	single	dual	plural
1	रामः [1/1]	रामौ [1/2]	रामाः [1/3]	Doer	मरुत्	मरुतौ	मरुतः
2	रामम् [2/1]	रामौ [2/2]	रामान्	Object	मरुतम्	मरुतौ	मरुतः [2/3]
3	रामेण [3/1]	रामाभ्याम्	रामैः [3/3]	By	मरुता	मरुद्भ्याम्	मरुद्भिः
4	रामाय [4/1]	रामाभ्याम्	रामेभ्यः	For	मरुते	मरुद्भ्याम्	मरुद्भ्यः
5	रामात् [5/1]	रामाभ्याम्	रामेभ्यः	From	मरुतः	मरुद्भ्याम्	मरुद्भ्यः
6	रामस्य [6/1]	रामयोः	रामाणाम्	Of	मरुतः	मरुतोः [6/2]	मरुताम्
7	रामे [7/1]	रामयोः	रामेषु [7/3]	In	मरुति	मरुतोः [7/2]	मरुत्सु
	हे राम	हे रामौ	हे रामाः	Hail	हे मरुत्	हे मरुतौ	हे मरुतः

Visarga undergoes many Sandhi changes, prominent is that it may become ओ, thus रामो instead of रामः । Also drops, thus मरुत instead of मरुतः । Anusvara is another common Sandhi. Thus रामं , रामाणां, मरुतं ।

As noticed in the verses, तिङन्त verbs are generally omitted or assumed intrinsically. There is more use of the क्त Past Passive Participle (ppp) as a verb. Full of 1st case Nominatives, 2nd case rare. There is frequent usage of the determinative TP Compound तत्पुरुषः समासः wherein the second or right side word is the main word.

In the Word Index, to highlight Sandhi and give a clue to the reader, final letter has been left in Sandhi modified form. E.g. verse 3.42 सम्बन्धसंयमाल् [5/1] Note that the correct spelling without Sandhi is सम्बन्धसंयमात् [5/1] and that has already been shown in the commentary.

3.43	अकल्पिता f1/1 (f for feminine)	2.5	अनित्याशुचिदुःखानात्मसु [7/3]
4.29	अकुसीदस्य 6/1	3.51	अनिष्टप्रसङ्गात् 5/1
3.54	अक्रमं n1/1 (n for neuter)	2.42	अनुत्तमसुखलाभः 1/1
3.45	अणिमादिप्रादुर्भावः [1/1]	1.11	अनुभूतविषयासंप्रमोषः [1/1]
1.8	अतद्रूपप्रतिष्ठम् n1/1	4.5	अनेकेषाम् n6/3
4.21	अतिप्रसङ्गः 1/1	3.7	अन्तरङ्गं n1/1
4.12	अतीतानागतं [n1/1]	1.30	अन्तरायाः 1/3
3.16	अतीतानागतज्ञानम् n1/1	1.29	अन्तरायाभावश् 1/1 च 0
3.35	अत्यन्तासंकीर्णयोः 7/2	3.21	अन्तर्धानम् n1/1
1.1	अथ [0] (0 for Indeclinable)	1.18	अन्यः 1/1
1.47	अध्यात्मप्रसादः 1/1	3.53	अन्यता f1/1
3.17	अध्यासात् 5/1	1.49	अन्यविषया f1/1
4.12	अध्वभेदाद् 5/1	1.50	अन्यसंस्कारप्रतिबन्धी 1/1 (प्रतिबन्धिन् m stem)
1.26	अनवच्छेदात् 5/1 , 3.53	3.22	अपरान्तज्ञानम् n1/1
2.22	अनष्टं n1/1 ppp verb	1.24	अपरामृष्टः 1/1
2.16	अनागतम् [n1/1 ppp verb]	2.39	अपरिग्रहस्थैर्ये [n7/1]
4.10	अनादित्वं n1/1	4.18	अपरिणामित्वात् 5/1
4.6	अनाशयम् n1/1		

1.26 अपि 0 , 1.29, 2.9, 2.20, 2.22, 3.50, 4.9, 4.24, 4.29

4.22 अप्रतिसंक्रमायास् f5/1

4.3 अप्रयोजकं n1/1

1.10 अभावप्रत्ययालम्बना f1/1 (feminine)

4.11 अभावे 7/1

1.41 अभिजातस्य 6/1

2.9 अभिनिवेशः 1/1

3.9 अभिभवप्रादुर्भावौ 1/2

1.39 अभिमतध्यानाद् 5/1 वा 0

4.8 अभिव्यक्तिर् f1/1

1.13 अभ्यासः 1/1

1.12 अभ्यासवैराग्याभ्यां n3/2

3.22 अरिष्टेभ्यो 5/3 Visargasandhi

1.28 अर्थभावनम् n1/1 ppp

1.43 अर्थमात्रनिर्भासा f1/1

1.45 अलिङ्गपर्यवसानम् n1/1

4.31 अल्पम् n1/1

1.3 अवस्थानम् n1/1

2.4 अविद्या f1/1 , 2.5, 2.24

2.3 अविद्यास्मितारागद्वेषाभिनिवेशाः 1/3

2.26 अविप्लवा f1/1

3.20 अविषयीभूतत्वात् 5/1

4.7 अशुक्लाकृष्णं n1/1

2.43 अशुद्धिक्षयात् 5/1

2.28 अशुद्धिक्षये 7/1

2.29 अष्टावङ्गानि n1/3

2.40 असंसर्गः 1/1

3.39 असङ्ग 1/1 visarga drop

4.12 अस्ति iii/1 लट् Verb

2.37 अस्तेयप्रतिष्ठायां f7/1

2.6 अस्मिता f1/1

4.4 अस्मितामात्रात् 5/1

1.40 अस्य 6/1

2.35 अहिंसाप्रतिष्ठायां f7/1

2.30 अहिंसासत्यास्तेयब्रह्मचर्यापरिग्रहा 1/3 visarga

2.28 आ 0

4.22 आकारापत्तौ f7/1

3.42 आकाशगमनम् n1/1

4.25 आत्मभावभावनाविनिवृत्तिः f1/1

2.21 आत्मा 1/1 (आत्मन् m stem)

4.9 आनन्तर्यं n1/1

4.31 आनन्त्याज् 5/1 sandhi

3.5 आलोकः 1/1

4.10 आशिष: f6/1 (आशिस् stem)

2.46 आसनम् n1/1

1.21 आसन्नः 1/1

1.4 इतरत्र 0

3.17 इतरेतर 0

1.20 इतरेषाम् 6/3 , 4.7

2.34 इति 0 , 3.55, 4.34

3.47 इन्द्रियजयः 1/1

2.54 इन्द्रियाणाम् n6/3 , 2.55

1.41 इव 0 , 1.43, 2.6, 2.54, 3.3

2.44 इष्टदेवतासंप्रयोगः 1/1

1.24 ईश्वरः 1/1

2.45 ईश्वरप्रणिधानात् 5/1

1.23 ईश्वरप्रणिधानाद् 5/1 वा 0 जश्त्व sandhi

4.28 उक्तम् n1/1 (ppp verb)

3.39 उत्क्रान्तिश् 1/1 च 0 visarga sandhi

2.4 उत्तरेषां 6/3

1.35 उत्पन्ना f1/1

3.39 उदानजयाज् 5/1 sandhi

3.37 उपसर्गौ 1/3 visarga drop

4.20 उभयानवधारणम् [n1/1]

1.48 ऋतम्भरा [f1/1]

4.16 एकचित्ततन्त्रं [n1/1]

1.32 एकतत्त्वाभ्यासः 1/1

3.4 एकत्र 0

4.5 एकम् n1/1

4.9 एकरूपत्वात् [n5/1]

4.20 एकसमये 7/1

3.12 एकाग्रतापरिणामः 1/1

2.6 एकात्मता f1/1

1.31 एजयत्वश्वासप्रश्वासा 1/3 Visarga drop

1.44 एतयैव 0

3.13 एतेन 3/1

1.46 एव 0 , 2.15, 2.21, 4.8

4.11 एषाम् 6/3 , 4.28 एषां n6/3

3.30 कण्ठकूपे 7/1

3.18 करणात् 5/1

3.22 कर्म [n1/1] (कर्मन् [n] stem) , 4.7

2.12 कर्माशयो 1/1 (visarga)

3.21 कायरूपसंयमात् 5/1

3.29 कायव्यूहज्ञानम् [n1/1]

3.45 कायसंपत् [f1/1] , 3.46

3.42 कायाकाशयोः 7/2

2.43 कायेन्द्रियसिद्धिर् [f1/1]

1.26 कालेन 3/1

4.16 किं [n1/1]

3.31 कूर्मनाड्यां [f7/1]

2.34 कृतकारितानुमोदिता 1/3 visarga drop

2.22 कृतार्थं 0

4.32 कृतार्थानां 6/3

4.34 कैवल्यं [n1/1] (कैवल्य [n] stem)

4 कैवल्यपादः 1/1

4.26 कैवल्यप्राग्भारं [n1/1]

2.25 कैवल्यम् [n1/1] , 3.50, 3.55

4.33 क्रमः 1/1

3.15 क्रमान्यत्वं [n1/1]

2.36 क्रियाफलाश्रयत्वम् [n1/1]

2.1 क्रियायोगः 1/1

1.5 क्लिष्टाक्लिष्टाः 1/3

4.30 क्लेशकर्मनिवृत्तिः [f1/1]

1.24 क्लेशकर्मविपाकाशयैर् 3/3

2.2 क्लेशतनूकरणार्थश् 1/1 च 0

2.12 क्लेशमूलः 1/1

4.28 क्लेशवत् 0

2.3 क्लेशाः 1/3

3.52 क्षणतत्क्रमयोः 7/2

4.33 क्षणप्रतियोगी 1/1 (योगिन् [m] stem)

3.11 क्षयोदयौ 7/1

1.41 क्षीणवृत्तेर् [f6/1]

2.52 क्षीयते Verb iii/1 लट् passive

3.30 क्षुत्पिपासानिवृत्तिः [f1/1]

2.4 क्षेत्रम् n1/1

4.3 क्षेत्रिकवत् 0 (–वत् Indeclinable)

2.49 गतिविच्छेदः 1/1

2.19 गुणपर्वाणि [n1/3]

2.15 गुणवृत्तिविरोधाच् 5/1 च 0

1.16 गुणवैतृष्ण्यम् [n1/1]

4.13 गुणात्मानः 1/3 (आत्मन् [m] stem)

4.32 गुणानाम् 6/3 , 4.34 गुणानां 6/3

1.26	गुरुः [1/1]
3.47	ग्रहणस्वरूपास्मितान्वयार्थवत्त्वसंयमाद् [5/1]
1.41	ग्रहीतृग्रहणग्राह्येषु 7/3
1.44	च [0] , 1.45, 2.41, 2.53 , 3.20 , 3.22 , 3.49, 4.16, 4.10, 4.20
3.21	चक्षुःप्रकाशासंप्रयोगे [7/1]
2.51	चतुर्थः [1/1]
3.27	चन्द्रे [7/1]
4.34	चितिशक्तिर् [f1/1]
4.22	चितेर् [6/1 visarga]
1.33	चित्तप्रसादनम् n1/1
4.15	चित्तभेदात् [5/1]
1.37	चित्तम् [n1/1], 4.5, 4.23 , 4.26
1.30	चित्तविक्षेपास् [1/3]
4.18	चित्तवृत्तयस् f1/3
1.2	चित्तवृत्तिनिरोधः [1/1]
3.34	चित्तसंवित् [f1/1]
2.54	चित्तस्य [n6/1], 3.1, 3.11 , 3.12, 3.38, 4.17
4.21	चित्तान्तरदृश्ये [7/1]
4.24	चित्रम् n1/1
3.54	चेति [0 (च इति)]
4.27	छिद्रेषु [7/3]
2.39	जन्मकथंतासंबोधः [1/1]
4.1	जन्मौषधिमन्त्रतपःसमाधिजाः [1/3]
1.28	जपस् n1/1
3.39	जलपङ्ककण्टकादिषु 7/3
4.9	जातिदेशकालव्यवहितानाम् [6/3]
2.31	जातिदेशकालसमयानवच्छिन्नाः [1/3]
3.53	जातिलक्षणदेशैर् [3/3]
4.2	जात्यन्तरपरिणामः [1/1]
2.13	जात्यायुर्भोगाः [1/3]
3.36	जायन्ते Verb iii/3
4.17	ज्ञाताज्ञातम् [n1/1] (ppp verb)
4.18	ज्ञाताश [1/3]
2.28	ज्ञानदीप्तिर् [f1/1]
3.52	ज्ञानम् [n1/1] , 3.54 (neuter)
4.31	ज्ञानस्य [n6/1]
4.31	ज्ञेयम् n1/1
1.36	ज्योतिष्मती [f1/1] (feminine)
3.40	ज्वलनम् n1/1
4.27	तच्छिद्रेषु (तत् [n1/1] छिद्रेषु [7/3])
1.28	तज् [n1/1] sandhi
1.50	तज्ञः (तत् [n1/1] neuter जः [1/1] masculine)
3.5	तज्जयात् [5/1]
1.29	ततः [0] 2.52, 2.55, 3.12, 3.36, 3.43, 3.45, 3.53, 4.3, 4.30, 4.32
4.8	ततस् [0] visarga
2.48	ततो [0] (Visarga Sandhi) , 3.48
1.22	ततोऽपि (ततः [0] अपि [0])
3.20	तत् [n1/1] (mostly तद् due to जश्त्व Sandhi)

1.32 तत् n1/1 , 3.17, 3.20, 4.18, also first word in many TP compounds

1.16 तत्परं (तत् n1/1 परं n1/1) neuter

1.13 तत्र 0 1.25, 1.42, 1.48, 3.2, 4.6

3.22 तत्संयमाद् 5/1

2.35 तत्सन्निधौ 7/1

1.41 तत्स्थतदञ्जनतासमापत्तिः 1/1

4.19 तत्स्वाभासं n1/1 adjective

2.9 तथा 0 रूढो 1/1 Visarga

2.22 तदन्यसाधारणत्वात् 5/1 adjective

3.8 तदपि 0

4.16 तदप्रमाणकं n1/1

4.11 तदभावः 1/1

2.25 तदभावात् 5/1

2.21 तदर्थे 0

4.24 तदसंख्येयवासनाभिश् f3/3

1.3 तदा 0 4.16, 4.26, 4.31

4.17 तदुपरागापेक्षित्वाच् 5/1

3.3 तदेव 0 अर्थमात्रनिर्भासं n1/1

1.28 तद् n1/1 sandhi , 4.22

3.28 तद्गतिज्ञानम् n1/1

3.21 तद्ग्राह्यशक्तिस्तम्भे 7/1

3.45 तद्धर्मानभिघातश् 1/1 च 0

4.8 तद्विपाकानुगुणानाम् 6/3

2.13 तद्विपाको 1/1 Visarga

2.11 तद्वृत्तयः f1/3

3.50 तद्वैराग्याद् 5/1

1.12 तन् n1/1 निरोधः 1/1

2.1 तपःस्वाध्यायेश्वरप्रणिधानानि n1/3

2.43 तपसः 5/1

4.15 तयोर् 5/2 visarga

2.49 तस्मिन् 7/1

1.27 तस्य 6/1 2.24, 2.27, 3.6, 3.10, 3.20

1.51 तस्यापि 0 (तस्य 6/1 अपि 0)

1.46 ता 1/3 Visarga drop

3.54 तारकं n1/1

3.27 ताराव्यूहज्ञानम् n1/1

4.10 तासाम् f6/3

1.21 तीव्रसंवेगानाम् 6/3

1.14 तु 0

3.12 तुल्यप्रत्ययौ 1/2

3.53 तुल्ययोः 7/2

1.30 ते 1/3 , 2.10, 2.14, 3.37, 4.13

3.4 त्रयम् n1/1 , 3.7

4.7 त्रिविधम् n1/1

3.41 दिव्यं n1/1

1.14 दीर्घकालनैरन्तर्यसत्कारासेवितो 1/1 Visarga

1.31 दुःखदौर्मनस्याङ्गम n1/1

2.15 दुःखम् n1/1 , 2.16

2.34 दुःखाज्ञानानन्तफला 1/3 Visarga drop

2.8 दुःखानुशायी 1/1 (अनुशयिन् m stem)

2.6	दृग्दर्शनशक्त्योर् f6/2	3.28	ध्रुवे 7/1
1.14	दृढभूमिः f1/1	3.20	न 0 4.16, 4.19
2.20	दृशिमात्रः 1/1	2.22	नष्टम् n1/1
2.25	दृशेः f6/1	3.29	नाभिचक्रे n7/1
4.19	दृश्यत्वात् 5/1	4.10	नित्यत्वात् 5/1
2.18	दृश्यम् n1/1	2.5	नित्यशुचिसुखात्मख्यातिर् f1/1
2.21	दृश्यस्य 6/1	1.10	निद्रा f1/1
2.12	दृष्टादृष्टजन्मवेदनीयः 1/3	4.3	निमित्तम् n1/1
1.15	दृष्टानुश्रविकविषयवितृष्णस्य 6/1	2.32	नियमाः 1/3
2.50	देशकालसंख्याभिः f3/3	1.25	निरतिशयं n1/1
3.1	देशबन्धः 1/1	3.22	निरुपक्रमं n1/1 ppp verb
3.50	दोषबीजक्षये 7/1	3.9	निरोधक्षणचित्तान्वयो 1/1 visarga
2.20	द्रष्टा 1/1 (द्रष्टृ m stem)	3.9	निरोधपरिणामः 1/1
1.3	द्रष्टुः 6/1 (द्रष्टृ m stem)	1.51	निरोधे 7/1
2.17	द्रष्टृदृश्ययोः 6/2	1.51	निर्बीजः 1/1
4.23	द्रष्टृदृश्योपरक्तं n1/1	3.8	निर्बीजस्य 6/1
2.48	द्वन्द्वानभिघातः 1/1 ppp verb	4.4	निर्माणचित्तानि n1/3
2.8	द्वेषः 1/1	1.47	निर्विचारवैशारद्ये n7/1
4.29	धर्ममेघः 1/1	1.44	निर्विचारा f1/1
3.13	धर्मलक्षणावस्थापरिणामा 1/3 visarga drop	1.43	निर्वितर्का f1/1
4.12	धर्माणाम् 6/3	1.5	पञ्चतय्यः 1/1
3.14	धर्मी 1/1 (धर्मिन् m stem)	4.15	पन्थाः 1/3
3.1	धारणा f1/1	3.19	परचित्तज्ञानम् n1/1
2.53	धारणासु f7/3	2.55	परमा f1/1
4.6	ध्यानजम् n1/1	1.40	परमाणुपरममहत्त्वान्तः 1/1
3.2	ध्यानम् n1/1	3.38	परशरीरावेशः 1/1
2.11	ध्यानहेयास् 1/3	4.24	परार्थं n1/1

3.35 परार्थत्वात् 5/1

4.32 परिणामक्रमसमाप्तिर् f1/1 visarga

2.15 परिणामतापसंस्कारदुःखैर् n3/3

3.16 परिणामत्रयसंयमाद् 5/1

3.15 परिणामान्यत्वे n7/1

4.33 परिणामापरान्तनिर्ग्राह्यः 1/1

4.14 परिणामैकत्वाद् 5/1

2.50 परिदृष्टो 1/1 ppp verb, visarga

2.40 परैर् 3/3

2.14 पुण्यापुण्यहेतुत्वात् 5/1

3.12 पुनः 0 , 3.51 पुनर् 0

1.16 पुरुषख्यातेर् f5/1

3.35 पुरुषज्ञानम् n1/1

1.24 पुरुषविशेष 1/1 Visarga drop

4.18 पुरुषस्य 6/1

4.34 पुरुषार्थशून्यानां 6/3

3.18 पूर्वजातिज्ञानम् n1/1

3.7 पूर्वेभ्यः 5/3

1.26 पूर्वेषाम् 6/3

2.18 प्रकाशक्रियास्थितिशीलं n1/1

3.43 प्रकाशावरणक्षयः 1/1

2.52 प्रकाशावरणम् n1/1

4.3 प्रकृतीनां f6/3

4.2 प्रकृत्यापूरात् 5/1

3.38 प्रचारसंवेदनाच् 5/1 च 0

1.34 प्रच्छर्दनविधारणाभ्यां 3/2

1.48 प्रज्ञा f1/1 , 2.27, 3.5

1.27 प्रणवः 1/1

2.22 प्रति 0 adverb

2.33 प्रतिपक्षभावनम् 1/1 , 2.34

3.53 प्रतिपत्तिः f1/1

4.34 प्रतिप्रसवः 1/1

2.10 प्रतिप्रसवहेयाः 1/3 ppp verb

1.32 प्रतिषेधार्थम् n1/1

1.29 प्रत्यक्चेतनाधिगमः 1/1

1.7 प्रत्यक्षानुमानागमाः 1/3

3.19 प्रत्ययस्य 6/1

2.20 प्रत्ययानुपश्यः 1/1

4.27 प्रत्ययान्तराणि n1/3

3.35 प्रत्ययाविशेषो 1/1 visarga

3.2 प्रत्ययैकतानता f1/1

2.54 प्रत्याहारः 1/1

3.48 प्रधानजयश् 1/1 visarga च 0

4.18 प्रभोः6/1

1.6 प्रमाणविपर्ययविकल्पनिद्रास्मृतयः 1/3

1.7 प्रमाणानि n1/3

2.47 प्रयत्नशैथिल्यानन्त्यसमापत्तिभ्याम् f5/2

4.5 प्रयोजकं n1/1

3.17 प्रविभागसंयमात् 5/1

4.5 प्रवृत्तिभेदे 7/1

1.35 प्रवृत्तिर् f1/1

3.25 प्रवृत्त्यालोकन्यासात् 5/1

3.10 प्रशान्तवाहिता f1/1

4.29 प्रसंख्याने 7/1

2.4 प्रसुप्ततनुविच्छिन्नोदाराणाम् 6/3

1.34 प्राणस्य 6/1

2.49 प्राणायामः 1/1

3.36 प्रातिभश्रावणवेदनादर्शास्वादवार्ता f1/3 visarga drop

3.33 प्रातिभाद् 5/1 वा 0

2.27 प्रान्तभूमिः f1/1

3.38 बन्धकारणशैथिल्यात् 5/1

3.23 बलानि n1/3

3.24 बलेषु n7/3

3.43 बहिः 0

3.8 बहिरङ्गं n1/1

2.51 बाह्याभ्यन्तरविषयाक्षेपी 1/1 (आक्षेपिन् m stem)

2.50 बाह्याभ्यन्तरस्तम्भवृत्तिर् f1/1

4.21 बुद्धिबुद्धेर् f6/1

2.38 ब्रह्मचर्यप्रतिष्ठायां f7/1

1.19 भवप्रत्ययो 1/1 visarga

1.33 भावनातश् 0 (–तः indeclinable)

3.26 भुवनज्ञानं n1/1

3.44 भूतजयः 1/1

2.18 भूतेन्द्रियात्मकं n1/1

3.13 भूतेन्द्रियेषु n7/3

3.6 भूमिषु f7/3

3.35 भोगः 1/1

2.18 भोगापवर्गार्थं n1/1

1.41 मणेर् 6/1

1.35 मनसः n6/1 , 2.53 (मनस् n stem)

3.48 मनोजवित्वं n1/1

3.43 महाविदेहा f1/1

2.31 महाव्रतम् n1/1

1.8 मिथ्याज्ञानम् n1/1

3.32 मूर्धज्योतिषि 7/1 (ज्योतिस् m stem)

2.13 मूले 7/1

1.22 मृदुमध्याधिमात्रत्वात् 5/1

2.34 मृदुमध्याधिमात्रा 1/3 visarga drop

1.33 मैत्रीकरुणामुदितोपेक्षाणां f6/3

3.23 मैत्र्यादिषु 7/3

1.13 यत्नः 1/1

1.39 यथा 0

2.29 यमनियमासनप्राणायामप्रत्याहारधारणा-ध्यानसमाधयो 1/3 visarga

2.30 यमाः 1/3

1.2 योगः 1/1 (7c Root युजिर् योगे)

2.28 योगाङ्गानुष्ठानाद् n5/1

1.1 योगानुशासनम् n1/1

4.7 योगिनस् 6/1 visarga

2.53 योग्यता f1/1

2.7 रागः 1/1

3.46 रूपलावण्यबलवज्रसंहननत्वानि n1/3

3.42 लघुतूलसमापत्तेश् f5/1 च 0

2.34 लोभक्रोधमोहपूर्वका 1/3 visarga drop

4.3 वरणभेदः 1/1 तु 0

1.40 वशीकारः 1/1

1.15 वशीकारसंज्ञा f1/1

2.55 वश्यता f1/1

4.16 वस्तु n1/1 , 4.17

4.14 वस्तुतत्त्वम् n1/1

1.9 वस्तुशून्यो 1/1 visarga

1.34 वा 0 , 1.35, 1.36, 1.37, 1.38, 3.22, 4.34

1.27 वाचकः $^{1/1}$

4.8 वासनानाम् f6/3

3.48 विकरणभावः $^{1/1}$

1.9 विकल्पः $^{1/1}$

1.31 विक्षेपसहभुवः $^{1/1}$

2.33 वितर्कबाधने $^{7/1}$

1.17 वितर्कविचारानन्दास्मितारूपानुगमात् 5/1

2.34 वितर्का $^{1/3}$ visarga drop

2.9 विदुषः $^{6/1}$ (विद्वस् m stem)

1.19 विदेहप्रकृतिलयानाम् $^{6/3}$

3.6 विनियोगः $^{1/1}$

1.8 विपर्ययो $^{1/1}$ visarga

4.15 विभक्तः 1/1

3 **विभूतिपादः** 1/1

1.18 विरामप्रत्ययाभ्यासपूर्वः 1/1

2.26 विवेकख्यातिर् f1/1

2.28 विवेकख्यातेः f6/1

4.29 विवेकख्यातेर् f6/1 visarga

3.52 विवेकजं n1/1 ppp verb , 3.54

4.26 विवेकनिम्नं n1/1

2.15 विवेकिनः $^{6/1}$

1.22 विशेषः $^{1/1}$

4.25 विशेषदर्शिन् $^{6/1}$ visarga drop (दर्शिन् m stem)

1.49 विशेषार्थत्वात् $^{5/1}$

2.19 विशेषाविशेषलिङ्गमात्रालिङ्गानि $^{n1/3}$

1.36 विशोका $^{f1/1}$

1.35 विषयवती $^{f1/1}$

1.37 वीतरागविषयं $^{n1/1}$

2.38 वीर्यलाभः $^{1/1}$

1.5 वृत्तयः $^{f1/3}$

1.10 वृत्तिः $^{f1/1}$

3.43 वृत्तिर् f1/1 visarga

1.4 वृत्तिसारूप्यम् $^{n1/1}$

2.35 वैरत्यागः $^{1/1}$

1.15 वैराग्यम् $^{n1/1}$

4.13 व्यक्तसूक्ष्मा $^{1/3}$ visarga drop

1.44 व्याख्याता $^{f1/1}$

3.13 व्याख्याताः f1/3

1.30 व्याधिस्त्यानसंशयप्रमादालस्याविरति-भ्रान्तिदर्शनालब्धभूमिकत्वानवस्थितत्वानि $_{n1/3}$

3.9 व्युत्थाननिरोधसंस्कारयोर् 6/2

3.37 व्युत्थाने $^{7/1}$

1.9 शब्दज्ञानानुपाती $^{1/1}$ (अनुपातिन् m stem)

1.42 शब्दार्थज्ञानविकल्पैः $^{3/3}$

3.17 शब्दार्थप्रत्ययानाम् 6/3

3.14 शान्तोदिताव्यपदेश्यधर्मानुपाती $^{1/1}$

3.12 शान्तोदितौ $^{1/2}$

2.20 शुद्धः $^{1/1}$

3.55 शुद्धिसाम्ये $^{7/1}$

2.32 शौचसंतोषतपःस्वाध्यायेश्वरप्रणिधानानि $^{n1/3}$

2.40 शौचात् $^{n5/1}$

1.20 श्रद्धावीर्यस्मृतिसमाधिप्रज्ञापूर्वक $^{1/1}$ visarga drop

1.49 श्रुतानुमानप्रज्ञाभ्याम् f5/2

3.41 श्रोत्रम् n1/1

3.41 श्रोत्राकाशयोः n7/2

2.49 श्वासप्रश्वासयोर् 6/2

1.14 स 1/1 Visarga drops

3.17 संकरस् 1/1 visarga

1.42 संकीर्णा f1/1

4.11 संगृहीतत्वाद् 5/1

2.42 संतोषाद् 5/1

1.17 संप्रज्ञातः 1/1

3.41 संबन्धसंयमाद् 5/1

3.4 संयमः 1/1

3.26 संयमात् 5/1

3.52 संयमाद् 5/1

2.23 संयोगः 1/1

2.25 संयोगाभावो 1/1 visarga

2.17 संयोगो 1/1 visarga

1.50 संस्कारः 1/1

1.18 संस्कारशेषः 1/1

3.18 संस्कारसाक्षात् 5/1

3.10 संस्कारात् 5/1

4.27 संस्कारेभ्यः 5/3

4.24 संहत्यकारित्वात् n5/1

3.51 सञ्ज्ञस्मयाकरणं n1/1

2.13 सति 7/1 , 2.49

3.55 सत्त्वपुरुषयोः 6/2

3.35 सत्त्वपुरुषयोर् 6/2 visarga

3.49 सत्त्वपुरुषान्यताख्यातिमात्रस्य 6/1

2.41 सत्त्वशुद्धिसौमनस्यैकाग्र्येन्द्रियजयात्मदर्शनयोग्यत्वानि n1/3

2.36 सत्यप्रतिष्ठायां f7/1

4.18 सदा 0 adverb

2.27 सप्तधा f1/1

1.46 सबीजः 1/1

1.46 समाधिः 1/1 , 1.51, 3.3, 4.29

3.11 समाधिपरिणामः 1/1

1 **समाधिपादः 1/1**

2.2 समाधिभावनार्थः 1/1

2.45 समाधिसिद्धिर् f1/1

3.37 समाधौ f7/1

3.40 समानजयाज् 5/1 sandhi

1.42 समापत्तिः f1/1

3.42 सम्बन्धसंयमाल् 5/1

2.15 सर्वं n1/1 , 3.33 सर्वम् n1/1

1.25 सर्वज्ञबीजम् 1/1

3.49 सर्वज्ञातृत्वं n1/1

4.29 सर्वथा 0 adverb

3.54 सर्वथाविषयम् n1/1

1.51 सर्वनिरोधान् 5/1

3.49 सर्वभावाधिष्ठातृत्वं n1/1

3.17 सर्वभूतरुतज्ञानम् n1/1

2.37 सर्वरत्नोपस्थानम् n1/1

3.54 सर्वविषयं n1/1

3.11 सर्वार्थतैकाग्रतयोः f7/2

4.23 सर्वार्थम् n1/1

4.31 सर्वावरणमलापेतस्य 6/1

1.44 सविचारा f1/1

1.42 सवितर्का f1/1

2 **साधनपादः** 1/1

2.31 सार्वभौमा 1/3 visarga drop (सार्वभौम m stem)

3.20 सालम्बनं n1/1

3.32 सिद्धदर्शनम् n1/1

3.37 सिद्धयः f1/3

1.33 सुखदुःखपुण्यापुण्यविषयाणां 6/3

2.7 सुखानुशायी 1/1 (अनुशयिन् m stem)

1.45 सूक्ष्मविषयत्वं n1/1

1.44 सूक्ष्मविषया f1/1

3.25 सूक्ष्मव्यवहितविप्रकृष्टज्ञानम् n1/1

2.10 सूक्ष्माः 1/3

3.26 सूर्ये 7/1

3.22 सोपक्रमं n1/1 ppp verb

3.51 स्थान्युपनिमन्त्रणे n7/1

1.35 स्थितिनिबन्धिनी 1/1

1.13 स्थितौ f7/1

2.46 स्थिरसुखम् n1/1

3.44 स्थूलस्वरूपसूक्ष्मान्वयार्थवत्त्वसंयमाद् 5/1

3.31 स्थैर्यम् n1/1

1.11 स्मृतिः 1/1

1.43 स्मृतिपरिशुद्धौ 7/1

4.21 स्मृतिसंकरश् 1/1 visarga च 0

4.9 स्मृतिसंस्कारयोर् 6/2 visarga

4.16 स्यात् iii/1 विधिलिङ् Verb

1.38 स्वप्ननिद्राज्ञानालम्बनं n1/1

4.22 स्वबुद्धिसंवेदनम् n1/1

2.9 स्वरसवाही 1/1 (वाहिन् m stem)

4.12 स्वरूपतः 0 (–तः indeclinable)

4.34 स्वरूपप्रतिष्ठा f1/1

3.3 स्वरूपशून्यम् n1/1

1.43 स्वरूपशून्या f1/1

2.54 स्वरूपानुकार 1/1 visarga drop

1.3 स्वरूपे n7/1

2.23 स्वरूपोपलब्धिहेतुः 1/1

2.54 स्वविषयासंप्रयोगे 7/1

2.23 स्वस्वामिशक्त्योः f6/2

2.40 स्वाङ्गजुगुप्सा f1/1

2.44 स्वाध्यायाद् 5/1

3.35 स्वार्थसंयमात् 5/1

3.24 हस्तिबलादीनि n1/3

2.25 हानं n1/1 , 4.28 हानम् n1/1

2.26 हानोपायः 1/1

2.34 हिंसादयः 1/3

3.34 हृदये n7/1

4.11 हेतुफलाश्रयालम्बनैः 3/3

2.24 हेतुर् 1/1 , 3.15 हेतुः 1/1

2.16 हेयं n1/1 ppp verb

2.17 हेयहेतुः 1/1

2.14 ह्लादपरितापफलाः 1/3

The Sanskrit Alphabet

वर्णमाला

ॐ अ आ इ ई उ ऊ ऋ ॠ ऌ ॡ   ए ऐ ओ औ   अं अः

					The Shiva Sounds
क्	ख्	ग्	घ्	ङ्	
च्	छ्	ज्	झ्	ञ्	
ट्	ठ्	ड्	ढ्	ण्	The Brahma Sounds
त्	थ्	द्	ध्	न्	
प्	फ्	ब्	भ्	म्	The Vishnu Sounds
य् र् ल् व्		श् ष् स्		ह्	
अँ	ळ्		व्ह्		Vedic Sanskrit

Conjunct letters are used frequently क्ष ज्ञ श्र, while

Long ॡ is not noticed in literature. The Sanskrit alphabet is commonly written without a halant. Consonants cannot be uttered without a vowel. So in teaching, each consonant is supplied with अ so that it can be uttered. There are 56 letters in the Vedic Alphabet.

20 Vowels अ आ अ३ इ ई इ३ उ ऊ उ३ ऋ ॠ ऋ३ ऌ ल३ ए ऐ ए३ ओ औ ओ३

34 Consonants

क ख ग घ ङ
च छ ज झ ञ
ट ठ ड ढ ण
त थ द ध न
प फ ब भ म
य र ल व श ष स   ह and ळ

2 Ayogavahas अं अः

Pronunciation of Sanskrit Letters

उच्चारणम्

अ son आ father इ it ई beat उ full ऊ pool ऋ rhythm

ॠ marine ऌ revelry ॡ ए play ऐ aisle ओ go औ loud

अं Anusvara is pure nasal – close the lips – similar to म्

अः Visarga is Breath release like ह् and preceding vowel sound

e.g. Pronounce नमः as नमह , शान्तिः as शान्तिहि , विष्णुः as विष्णुहु

क seeK	ख Khan	ग Get	घ loGHut	ङ sing
च Chunk	छ catchhim	ज Jump	झ heDGEhog	ञ bunch
ट True	ठ anTHill	ड Drum	ढ goDHead	ण under
त Tamil	थ Thunder	द That	ध breaTHE	न nut
प Put	फ Fruit	ब Bin	भ abhor	म much

य loYal र Red ल Luck व Vase श Sure ष Shun स So Hum ह

Conjuncts in general – first utter the top part and then the bottom one, e.g.

Bhagavad Gita 10.16 तिष्ठसि -> ष् ठ ,

Bhagavad Gita 10.23 शङ्करश्चास्मि -> ङ् क , श् च

Specific Conjuncts

ह् ण = ह्ण , ह् न = ह्न , ह् म = ह्म

Utter with emphasis on the chest, first the nasal and then the aspiration, e.g. Brahma = ब्रह्म *Pronounce as **Bramha***

Place & Effort of Enunciation

Place of speech	Vowels स्वर		Row Consonants व्यञ्जन					Semi vow el	Sibi lant
			Alpaprana		Mahaprana				
	Short	Long	1st	2nd	3rd	4th	5th		
कण्ठ	अ	आ	क	ख	ग	घ	ङ		
तालु	इ	ई	च	छ	ज	झ	ञ	य	श
मूर्धा	ऋ	ॠ	ट	ठ	ड	ढ	ण	र	ष
दन्त	ऌ		त	थ	द	ध	न	ल	स
ओष्ठ	उ	ऊ	प	फ	ब	भ	म		

Consonants are supplied with vowel अ to aid enunciation

कण्ठ – तालु	ए	ऐ	Diphthongs have twin places of utterance, being compound vowels
कण्ठ – ओष्ठ	ओ	औ	
दन्त – ओष्ठ	व		The vakara is different from the other semivowels as it has twin places of utterance
नासिक्य	ं , अं		Anusvara is a pure Nasal
अनुनासिका	ँ , ॐ , यँ		Candrabindu means Nasalization
कण्ठ Soft, Mahaprana	ह		Hakara is an Aspirate. It is sounded like a soft release of breath
	ः		Visarga is an Aspirate. It is sounded like ह alongwith its preceding vowel

Ardha Visarga ः is also written as ⌧

Base of tongue Hard, Alpaprana	ः or ⌧	Jihvamuliya pronounce as ह् (a visarga preceding क , ख)
ओष्ठ Hard, Alpaprana	ः or ⌧	Upadhmaniya pronounce as फ् (a visarga preceding प , फ)

अ	आ	इ	ई	उ	ऊ	ऋ	ॠ	ऌ	
a	ā	i	ī	u	ū	ṛ	ṝ	l̥	
					꣹	꣹	꣹		
ए	ऐ	ओ	औ	◌ं	◌ँ	◌:		✕	
ē	ai	ō	au	ṁ	m̐	ḥ		Ardha visarga	

Consonants are shown with vowel a = अ for uttering

क	ख	ग	घ	ङ		Consonant only with halant			
ka	kha	ga	gha	ṅa		क्अ = क		ka	
च	छ	ज	झ	ञ			क्	k	
ca	cha	ja	jha	ña					
ट	ठ	ड	ढ	ण					
ṭa	ṭha	ḍa	ḍha	ṇa					
त	थ	द	ध	न					
ta	tha	da	dha	na					
प	फ	ब	भ	म					
pa	pha	ba	bha	ma					
य	र	ल	व						
ya	ra	la	va						
श	ष	स	ह		ळ	s	avagraha		
śa	ṣa	sa	ha		ḷa	'			

Halant ◌् is not a separate character in the transliteration. It simply means lack of vowel in the consonant.

e.g. Both these words end in "n" but one has a halant in Devanagari. So the word without the halant has a vowel added to it in transliteration. E.g. Arjuna अर्जुन śrī bhagavān श्री भगवान्

The ISO 15919 standard
https://www.iso.org/standard/28333.html

References

Author	Title	Edition	Year	Publisher
Sri Sri Ravi Shankar	Patanjali Yoga Sutras	1st	2010	Sri Sri Publications Trust, Bangalore
Tookaram Tatya	The Yoga Philosophy	2nd	1885	The Theosophical Society, Bombay
Hari Narayan Apte	पातञ्जलयोगसूत्राणि	1st	1904	Ananda Ashram, Pune
Christopher Chapple, Yogi Anand Viraj	The Yoga Sutras of Patanjali – An analysis of the Sanskrit	1st	1990	Sri Satguru Publications, Delhi
Swami Vivekananda	Raja Yoga: Conquering the Internal Nature	1st	1998	Advaita Ashrama Kolkata
Surinder Shanker Anand	पातञ्जल योग (अष्टाङ्गयोग)	1st	2006	Surinder Shanker Anand, Chandigarh
Sri Swami Satchidananda	The Yoga Sutras of Patanjali (Revised)	1st	2012	Integral Yoga Publications, Buckingham, Virginia
A. K. Aruna	Patanjali Yoga Sutras	1st	2012	Upasana Yoga Media, Palm Desert, California
Gabriel Pradipaka	Pātañjalayogasūtra-s	https://www.sanskrit-trikashaivism.com/		
Charles Johnston	The Yoga Sutras of Patanjali	http://www.gutenberg.org/ebooks/2526		
K. L. V. Sastry, AnantaramaSastri	Sabda Manjari (1961) Reprint	1st	2013	R. S. Vadhyar & Sons, Palghat
Ashwini Kumar Aggarwal	Dhatupatha Verbs in 5 Lakaras Vol1, 2, 3	1st	2017	Devotees of Sri Sri Ravi Shankar Ashram, Punjab
	Maheshwar Sutras Pratyaharas	1st	2018	

Transliteration
https://www.ashtangayoga.info/sanskrit/transliteration/translitera
tion-tool/#devanagari/iso15919/

http://yogasutrastudy.info/yoga-sutra-translations/ysp-in-
devanagari-sanskrit/

Spoken Sanskrit http://spokensanskrit.org/

Sanskrit Documents
https://sanskritdocuments.org/sanskrit/upanishhat/

Yoga Sutra Audio
https://sadvidyafoundation.org/online-lessons/yoga-sutra-
chanting/yoga-sutra-level-1-chapter-1/

Abhyaasa App https://www.abhyaasa.com/

Sattva App https://www.sattva.life/

Agnistoma All World Gayatri Parivar
http://literature.awgp.org/akhandjyoti/1956/January/v2.18

Deep Relaxation - Sama Veda The Art of Living
https://www.youtube.com/watch?v=xv0RdrEl3rA

What is the Main purpose of Yoga?
https://www.youtube.com/watch?v=ptRx712n-sc

Krishan Verma https://shudham.org/

Asana Pranayama

Asana and Pranayama are always learnt from a qualified Acharya.

Surya Namaskar is a favourite asana practice.
https://www.artofliving.org/in-en/yoga/yoga-poses/sun-salutation

Padmasadhana is definitely top of the world.
https://www.artofliving.org/yoga/yoga-poses/padma-sadhana
https://www.youtube.com/watch?v=4EBswVUU3po

Anulom Vilom Pranayama, also called Nadi Shodhan, is again a beneficial pranayama for all.
https://www.artofliving.org/yoga/breathing-techniques/alternate-nostril-breathing-nadi-shodhan

Slow chant Om Namah Shivaya Pranayama surely gets you there.
https://www.youtube.com/watch?v=kf_2sh-kMyU

The Tamil Siddha Bogar

Bogar is hailed as one of the 18 Tamil Siddhas, who lived may thousands of years ago. His place is the town of Palani in Tamil Nadu. His areas of expertise match those of Patanjali, viz. Yoga, Ayurveda and Language.
Bogar pranayama consists of पूरक–अंतर कुम्भक–रेचक–भाह्य कुम्भक
Inhalation:Retention:Exhalation:Retention in the count of 2:4:1:4
Always breathe-In from left nostril, breathe-Out from right nostril.

Agnistoma

Hymns of the Sama Veda which eulogise Agni are called Agnistoma. The agnistoma is the first of the soma yajnas It is spread over five days involving sixteen priests and is also called jyotistoma as many hymns have the sound 'Jyoti ' (Light). The burning kundalini force rising from the mooladhara chakra is met by the cool nourishing drops of nectar from the sahasrara in this vedic ritual. Listening to Sama Veda chants once a week is good enough.

Many Yogis have enriched, enhanced and made my life blossom.
Discover the Yogi in your life, seek blessings and taste liberation.

Sri Sri Ravi Shankar
BholeBaba_JaniMuni Kanwal_Maa Ludhiana
Surindar Kavita Munilal Kailash Kishanchand Satyavati Ludhiana
Sarvjit Mohali
KrishanVerma Amol Purshu Samir Meenal Neeraj Bangalore Ashram
Banka Rupan Puneet Ardamanbir Vandana Manoj Jagjit Ludhiana
Mukund Arun Maitreyee Mumbai
Rajesh Prateek Stanley Rewari
Somnath Shilajeet Nitin Monica Kinkini Vasudha Ambernath
Yashoda Priyadarshini Ganesh TamilNadu
Mandeep Willey Sangeeta Uppi Patiala
Tarun Gudiya Ranchi
Shambhu Dass Surekha Vimal Disha Pilani
NarayanSingh Barkha Faridabad
Shree_Shree_Maa Prakash Ahmedabad
Nandita Atul Bathinda
Rochak Delhi
Bhandari KJ KP DP Saini Tikku Harish ShivajiDas Thapar College
Omkar Govt. College
Spykar Univ. of Saskatchewan
Ruth Darrell John Lisa Regiers Leyton Bernis Saskatoon
Gjermund Ellen Erik Seamus Suzanne Jason Swarna Oslo
Sanjay Synergy Systems Vinod Drammen
Suzi England
Valerie Paris
Hemswaroop Vahelal

The layers of ignorance are Real, ordinary and Correctable. Dust on mirror is wipeable.

<u>Techniques are simple Time is available</u>

Using Sudanta toothpaste and Dant kanti toothpowder and occasional Neem datun for twice a day brushing
Washing eyes with Triphala water and doing sunning

Playing on the Playground and going for Long walks

Reflexology and Oil Massage Pancakarma

Haritaki and Triphala, Homa Ash and desi gaumutra

PlantingTrees WateringPlants TalkingtoFlowers
Living in Vaastu homes and reducing plastic and app use
Refraining from complaints does it all. <u>Nature is kind</u>

सर्वे भवन्तु सुखिनः । सर्वे सन्तु निरामयाः ।
सर्वे भद्राणि पश्यन्तु । मा कश्चिद् दुःख भाग् भवेत् ॥
ॐ शान्तिः शान्तिः शान्तिः

When faith has blossomed in life, Every step is led by the Divine.

Sri Sri Ravi Shankar

Om Namah Shivaya

जय गुरुदेव

9 789353 116576